CONTENTS

PREFACE

Anyone who wishes to take his or her communal religious faith seriously, has to deal with the issues of religious authority and its role in the development of one's faith.

In the ecclesiology courses that I have taught in the last four years to graduate students as well as undergraduate students, the issue of authority in the Church has been a constant and often controversial topic of discussion. While most students viewed church authority with the kind of cynicism they have toward all institutional authority, a few of them regarded obedience to ecclesiastical authorities, especially to the Pope, as an essential element of their catholic faith. While many contemporary catholics view obedience to authority as arcane, demeaning and insulting to a person's autonomy, others profess that allegiance to the legitimate authorities, especially the papacy, is the essence of catholicism.

In view of my familiarity with, and knowledge of catholic theology, I have discussed the issue of authority in the context of the catholic tradition. However, the historical survey and the fundamental theological perspectives presented in this work can be valid, in my view, to anyone who wishes to make sense of authority, to one's own communal religious faith.

I have written this book having in mind college students and those preparing for careers in the Church ministry. This is not, in a strict sense, a scholarly treatise on authority, although it does have a scholarly basis.

.

ACKNOWLEDGEMENTS

I wish to thank my teachers in undergraduate studies especially Reverends Antonio D'Souza, Francis Diniz, John Pereira and Alex Gracias who encouraged me in my studies of philosophy and theology.

I wish to thank also all my teachers in graduate studies at Marquette University, in Milwaukee, whose presence in my life, and whose ideas and even idiosyncracies elicited in me reflections on the subject matter of this work. None of them however, are responsible for anything that I have written in this book.

INTRODUCTION

In the Catholic tradition, members of the Church have been urged to see God in the officers of the Church, and the will of God in their commands. For the power of the ruler is seen as God's own ruling power, bestowed upon the ruler. [1]

Christ is alleged to have established a divine power which he gave at the beginning to Peter as his "vicar" on earth, and that power was handed down to those who came after him in a historical sequence of transmission and succession. The Pope now is the vicar, the visible Christ, and that everyone in the hierarchy shares to some extent in the divinely established power.

The first section of this work is devoted to provide a summary background of the historical processes in the context of which the Church appropriated a sociopolitical self-understanding as a *societas perfecta*, (perfect society) a society constituted under the monarchical rule of the successor of Peter. Under the pressure of two series of events, namely, the struggle with political powers, and the struggle with the spiritualistic movements within the Church, and later with the Reformation, which attacked its worldly interests and power structures, the Church, in turn, accentuated its juridical and visible reality. Authority within this sociopolitical perspective, amounted to the rule of clerics over the laity. Influential treatises on ecclesiology, especially those that followed the Gregorian Reform of the 11th century legitimized the juridical vision of the Church, which was reinforced in subsequent centuries and reached its apogee by the time of Vatican Council One in the 19th century. From the historical survey, it will be obvious that the sociopolitical self-understanding of the Church and its authority, developed in response to historical realities.

This study holds that the essential reality of the Church has evolved through various forms of historical manifestations, and its self-understanding was shaped by a concrete milieu. As the scholar of history Emile Poulat rightly observes: "For the Church, history (as it constitutes itself) is the location of its self-understanding."2

History also helps us to distinguish the essential from the accidental , as Yves Congar rightly points out: "Through familiarity with historical forms we can distinguish more clearly the permanence of the essential and the variation of forms; we can locate the absolute and the relative more exactly, and so better remain true to the absolute while we shape the relative to the needs of the time." 3 Knowledge of history makes possible a healthy relativism, and helps us to de-mythologize our vision of reality, and, in our case the view of the Church.

In the second section, I have attempted to present a non-sociopolitical concept of authority. The traditional classicist theology erred because it conceived Church after the likeness of a body politic, and articulated the concept of authority based on political theories. But Church is first and foremost the *locus* and the sign of God's abiding presence amidst us. Therefore, the concept of authority should be derived from this essential reality, rather than from its institutional similarities with a body politic.

Furthermore conceptions of the church based on socio-political models, betray the "essential nature" of the Church. I suggest that in formulating a theory of authority, we place it in the context of Christian Economy (Oikonomia)[4], characterized by God's self-giving in spirit and grace, and wherein the visible Church is a permanent expression of that economy of grace. As a consequence: 1) every kind of authority in the Church has to be, in effect, *the power of grace and love, the authority of the Spirit itself shining through human channels.* Such authority is not confined to the official hierarchical structure; it is the type of authority to be found among all those who are purely and simply godly persons; those who are genuinely spiritual people and friends of God. The power that a spiritual person has, is the power of God's grace operative in him or her. The authority in the Church, therefore, is primarily of "spiritual" nature and not of "juridical" nature. 2) The Church, however, will always be in need of an organizational structure and an institutional governing organ. But the institutional reality does not have ultimacy of its own, but ought to derive its significance from the essential reality of the Church, the reality of God's presence operative in grace and spirit. The entire institutional reality, and specifically the juridical element of authority is called to be a sign and instrument, a "sacrament" of the power of Spirit, grace and love. Considered this way, the theory of authority in Church is drawn from spiritual anthropology, rather than from political theories.

In opposition to the monarchical notion of the past, there is a tendency nowadays to promote a democratic notion of authority as an ideal form of authority in the Church. With growing appreciation of democratic spirit and democratic structures, there is a tendency to justify the latter as being of divine character. But this position falls, once again, into the same error as that of classicist theology, of defining Church as a body politic, with the only difference being, that the source of power now would be the people (*demos*), rather than the monarch.

It is true that a democratic view of authority entails a set of ethical and humanistic ideals which can be well used to signify the power of grace and love. But we should avoid falling prey to the temptation of drawing a notion of authority in the Church, based on political theories. By attempting to redefine authority in Church by means of harmonizing it with a political theory, we reduce Church to the likeness of State, as the classicist position had done.

The American scripture scholar, John L. McKenzie, commenting on this issue, rightly observed that authority in the Church is neither absolute, nor democratic, but unique in character.[5] It is this "unique" non-political vision that we need to strive to articulate. This work contains a modest attempt to articulate one type of a non-political notion of authority in the Church.

SECTION I:
A HISTORICAL SURVEY

1. HISTORICAL CONTEXT

The Church like any other organization has to be viewed as an open system in constant interaction with its environment, and the kind of interactions which take place exert a direct influence on its self-understanding. Historians and social analysts have articulated that interaction as a process of assimilation or integration by the Church of its surrounding environment. Without denying the existence of this process this study accepts another process that is characteristic of any organization, a process by which the self-understanding of the organization is also shaped by its defensive responses to real or perceived threats. Works in the sociology of organizations shed light on the structures that result in large part as a cumulative organizational response to a threatening environment.[1] By means of a brief historical review, this study intends to frame a context in which the Church appropriated a self-understanding of a socio-political nature, as a self-sufficing juridical entity.

The Church of the Roman Empire

The primitive Church was a loose assemblage of quasi-autonomous communities. In the pre-Nicene centuries "the local ecclesia was largely self-sufficient and to a surprising degree autonomous. Unity among churches manifested itself in agreement on faith rather than in institutional structures. In fact, no permanent organizational machinery existed above the level of the local church."[2] One faith in the Risen Christ united the scattered congregations.

The first threats to these faith-bound communities came in the form of schisms and heresies that grew out of Judaizing movements. The most serious challenge came from Gnosticism, a doctrine that stressed, among other things, the salvation through *gnosis* or knowledge. Influenced by Gnostic mythology, Marcion began advocating a Christian faith divorced from and even hostile to the Old Testament. Other doctrines like those of Montanism and Docetism and other minor heresies began disintegrating the original faith-communities. The immediate challenge to the Church was how to stop its members from being lost to other sects and heresies. The Church responded by stressing the apostolic succession of bishops as the criterion for doctrinal genuineness. Thus, the role of the bishop to define the doctrines and uphold their uniformity became prominent. In fact, the three "criteria of apostolic continuity" - apostolic Scripture, apostolic tradition, and apostolic episcopate - interacted with one another to form the standard of Christian truth and the "rule of faith." Hence, the social structure of the Church no less than the creed and doctrine of the Church was defined in terms of its continuity with the apostles.[3] Briefly, the heresies gave the Church an impetus to organize itself in terms of a systematic formulation of doctrines and to the acknowledgement of the bishops as the guardians of orthodoxy.

The conversion of Emperor Constantine in 312 led to further demands on the Church for an organizational machinery. The imperial favor bolstered a flood of converts to the faith and the Church experienced a rapid growth in membership, requiring thereby a more complex coordination. Constantine, for his part, had an interest in a unified and well-organized Church. As an experienced political leader, he saw in the Church a highly effective means of promoting internal cohesion and he looked for a close collaboration of Church with the State in the interest of imperial unity. He saw Christianity as a most potent factor in cementing the Empire.

Constantine did not interfere in the internal affairs of the Church, except when the internal dissensions affected the unity and peace within the Empire, such as in the Arian controversy. The Church, for its part, had a positive estimation of the Roman Empire, ascribing to it a providential mission for the spread of Christian faith.

Although the merger with the Empire strengthened the Church, the marriage of *regnum* and *sacerdotium* (kingdom and priesthood) was soon to prove troublesome. Constantine's son, Constantius, wished to exercise direct control over the Church and went to the point of demanding a complete subjection of the Church to the State: "It was to be a State-Church incorporated into the *Imperium*, whose absolute sovereign was the Emperor."4 He sent into exile those bishops who opposed his supremacy in church affairs. The resistance to the Emperor was led by Athanasius of Alexandria and he was the first bishop of the 4th century to formulate the Church's claim to freedom vis-a-vis the State.5 "*Christianitas*" in the 4th century as the "Church of the Empire," on the one hand incorporated ideas and structures of "*Romanitas*," while on the other hand, it lived in an ongoing tension with the Roman imperial power.

In the process of evangelization of the Roman Empire, the Church came face to face with social structures, economic realities and forms of cultural life of the society. In regards to marriage and family life, the Church accepted the existing laws of marriage and gave a spiritual significance to marital union. While Roman law denied any juridical worth to marriage between slaves, the Church regarded them as valid. Various other provisions regarding the marriages of the slaves were altered under the Christian leadership. The Church also changed the meaning and extent of the rights of the *paterfamilias* over the contracting of marriage by his children; it wanted this to be understood not so much as a right but rather as concern for the child. Laws defining the relations of the married couples were altered so as to bring fairness to both.[6] The Church did not in principle question the prevailing economic system or the basic structures of contemporary society. It did not, for instance, advocate rejection of slavery, for it even saw it as a necessary element of the contemporary economic order. However, the Church stood up more decisively for the alleviation of the lot of slaves. If master and slave were Christians, it used the leverage of their one faith to relax the relationship of domination by preaching that all the baptized are children of one heavenly Father. Karl Baus notes: "it was due to the influence of the Church that from the fourth century the emancipation of slaves grew to a considerable extent."[7] In the year 331 the Church was also given the right to emancipate slaves, with all the legal consequences, by a special act within the church building.

As regards the ownership of property and wealth, the Church accepted the right of private property, in spite of the overwhelmingly unequal distribution of property. Yet, the Church Fathers relentlessly condemned the behavior of rich people and the methods and practices that had become common in economic and commercial life. They led a bitter struggle against every form of overcharging in business, like high interests on loans. A synod in Carthage in 401 even asked the Emperor to appoint *defensores* to protect the poor from the encroachment of the rich.[8]

Seeing rampant misery, the Church initiated social welfare programs. This work was supported by the community, and the local bishop was ultimately responsible for it; a deacon was entrusted with direct administration, having deaconessess and widows to help him to conduct the program. The local churches established houses to take care of the sick and aid the poor and the orphans. There were also inns for "foreigners" passing through; this service was regarded as an *officium hospitalitatis* (duty of hospitality) of each bishop. Hospitals were erected for the needy all over the Christian regions, and hotels for strangers. The Church extended its charitable care also for captives and prisoners.

In the cultural life of the Roman Empire, there was a gradual infiltration of Christian ideals, images and ideas which came from the world of the Bible. The Christian standards of value and ways of life were being constantly impressed upon the converts. Thus Christianity began to influence minds of the individuals and social groups. By the middle of the fifth century the Church through its relentless missionary activity had reached to all corners of the Empire and the people professed and felt themselves to be Christians, except for a few groups and tribes.

The symbiosis produced not only a fusion of ideas, but even a fusion of structures. Reflections of the Empire could be seen in every aspect of the Christian Church and vice-versa. The provincial structure of the Church and its hierarchical order of command was based on that of the Empire. The Council of Chalcedon (451) even decreed that the Church should adapt its organization to conform to changes in the civil organization. Similarly the papal chancery was modelled on its imperial counterpart, in its methods, documents, and other procedures. This process of assimilation of *Romanitas* by the Church continued more vigorously in the course of centuries.[9]

On the other hand, there was an ongoing tension present between the Church and the Empire. The Church experienced an encroachment by the Empire on its ecclesiastical domain, especially in matters of defining doctrine and morals. The Church was already a power to reckon with, having wielded enormous influence on the social, economic and cultural life of the population, and among the Fathers of the Church there were those who relentlessly fought to defend the autonomy of the Church against the encroachments of the Emperors.

As a result, the characteristic position developed by great Christian thinkers like Ambrose (IV c.) and Augustine (V c.) and later Gregory the Great (VI c.) was that human society was divinely ordained to be ruled by a dual organization, each having a distinguishable jurisdiction. The Church ruled in matters of eternal salvation and spiritual interests, while the civil government controlled the temporal interests and the maintenance of peace and order. Humankind formed a single society divinely ordained to be governed by two authorities, the spiritual and the temporal, the one wielded by priests and the other by secular rulers. This view came to be known as the doctrine of the two swords, which received authoritative expression from Pope Gelasius I at the close of the 5th century. In this conception, the Church was as universal as the Empire, for both included all persons. The Church was not a distinct group of persons joined together by a voluntary acceptance of the Christian doctrine, as is conventionally understood in modern times. All humankind formed a single Christian society ruled by two governments each with its own law, its own organs of legislation and administration, the spiritual rule of priests and the temporal rule of kings.[10]

The Church in Post-Imperial Period

Because of the changing political, social and economic situation of the time, the period after the fall of the Western Roman Empire (476) is of great significance in the development of the image of the Church. A combination of various elements such as continuous barbarian pressure on long, exposed frontiers of the Empire, a stagnating economic system, weak leadership and other factors led to the downfall of the Western Roman Empire. One after another its provinces fell and the sovereignty technically reverted to the Eastern Roman Emperor.[11] The Church had a peaceful cohabitation under Theodoric, the head of the Ostrogroths, who scrupulously respected the jurisdictional rights of the Church. The imperial reconquest of Italy brought in an Eastern military governor, eventually to be called the exarch of Ravenna. The Roman Church soon lost the freedom it had enjoyed under Theodoric. The rulers interferd in the administrative and doctrinal affairs of the Church which even led to what came to be known as the

Istrian schism. In the year 568 the Lombards struck again and from then onwards, the history of the Western Roman empire is "one of successive advances and retreats, sieges and reliefs, truces and treaties, which constitute a gradual process of erosion of imperial territory."[12]

During this period of political upheaval, the papacy had to fight its own battle for survival and recovery. There was the intermittent warfare between the imperial and Lombard forces, and the Church often played the role of an ally to one or the other by providing material help as well as by using its moral authority to appeal for aid and support. The Roman Church on the one hand, believed in itself as the bastion of orthodoxy in matters of doctrine and morals; on the other hand, it saw itself closely linked to the Roman Empire. The ecclesiastical politics became muddled with East-West imperial interest. Relations between Rome and Constantinople got markedly worse. The promulgation of Emperor Zeno's Henotikon in 482 was clearly seen as an attempt by the emperors to alter the faith without recourse to church council. Pope Felix II (483), with no desire to cause a breach with the Eastern Church urged the Emperor to respect the Chalcedonian provision and asked Patriarch Acacius to remain faithful to Chalcedon. The papal pleas fell on deaf ears and the controversy eventually resulted in a schism.

Whatever the nature of the relations between Roman Church and the barbarian states, the latter accorded the former due respect. The Lombard Kings, as they gradually became civilized and embraced Christian faith, regarded the pope as the patriarch of the Western Church and, to a certain extent, as an ally in their struggle with the Eastern Empire.[13]

The social and economic situation after the fall of the Western Roman Empire can be evaluated from a famous passage of Pope Gregory the Great, written soon after his accession in 590:

> What happiness is there left in the world? Everywhere we
> see war. Everywhere we hear groans. Our cities are dest-
> royed; our fortresses are overthrown; our fields laid waste;

> the land is become a desert. No inhabitants remain in the countryside,scarcely is any in the towns. The small remnant of humanity surviving is daily and without cease borne down. Yet the scourge of divine justice has no end....Some we have seen led into captivity, others mutilated, others killed. So what happiness is there left in the world? See to what strait Rome, once mistress of the world, is reduced. Worn down by her great and ceaseless sorrows, by the loss of her citizens, by the assault of the enemy, by the frequency of ruin--thus we see brought to pass the sentence long ago pronounced on the city of Samaria by the prophet Ezekiel. [14]

The permanent state of warfare during the barbaric invasions and the imperial reconquest created a chaotic situation for the population of the Empire. The destruction which occurred during the Gothic wars (ca. 536-554) alone was beyond description. The provinces, plagued with immense destruction, famine and depletion of resources, were reeling in misery. Gregory the Great's *Dialogi* record the destruction of groups as well as individuals. Large sections of the population fled desperately seeking for war-free safety zones, and this situation led to reorganizing the bishoprics because their populations had been reduced.

Furthermore, this chaotic period coincides with the onset of a plague affecting entire regions and populations between the year 540 to 760. The plague seems to have originated in Northern Africa and spread through the east, ravaging Italy and France in intermittent waves. It is estimated that it "probably caused as large a mortality in the empire as the Black Death of the 14th century."[15] Its symptoms were similar to Black Death: fever, hallucinations and a swelling in the groin or armpit. The effects of this plague were so serious that those who were infected could not carry on with the routine of everyday life.

In the face of the considerable social and economic disasters, the starved and the oppressed populace turned en masse toward the Church. In Rome the papacy took over the social services, and from the mid-sixth century onwards, the Church was systematically undertaking the feeding of the people and the relief work for the needy. By the time of Gregory the Great, the Church had organized its welfare and charitable programs on proper administrative lines.[16] There were registers kept of the aid received and the revenues distributed by the Church in kind, such as grain, wine, cheese, vegetables, fish, and oil. Gregory the Great had even established mobile meals service for the sick. The charitable work of the Church extended to all levels of society. Under these chaotic social, political and economic circumstances, the Roman Church came to be looked upon as the agency of welfare and service to the distraught populace, as the bulwark of order and discipline and as a solace for every kind of human tribulation. The bishops and the pope came to be regarded by people as natural leaders who responded to their needs in a way that imperial government was not able to. The personality of some church leaders, such as Gregory the Great, helped to wield further influence for the Church; he extended his papacy much beyond the purely ecclesiastical affairs by negotiating political treaties, appointing commanders and even dispatching troops to protect Rome from the Lombardic invasions. The Roman Church during this period, carried on some of the functions of the Roman Empire.

Politically, Rome was dissociated from the ancient Empire, which had become a Greek state. Yet, for its contemporaries, the Empire was not only a political but also a spiritual reality. The popes stood for and spoke for ecclesiastical entity but always within the Empire as its substratum of unity.

The concept of the unity of Christendom became a reality once again in the Carolingian Empire. The anointing of Pepin as King by Pope Boniface was of decisive importance for the development of the Christian notion of the king in the West; the royal anointing came to be regarded as a sacrament and the ruler's position in the Church became ritually legitimatized. The coronation of Charles the Great by Pope Leo III in the year 800 and his acclamation as the Roman Emperor, adopted the Roman - Christian imperial ideology wherein the imperial office was defined as dominion over Christendom. Charles' new imperial title was *Karolus serenissimus Augustus, a Deo coronatus, magnus et pacificus imperator, Romanum gubernans imperium, qui est per misericordiam Dei rex Francorum et Longobardorum*[17] (Charles, the most serene Augustus, crowned by God, mighty and peaceful emperor, governing the Roman empire, who is, by the mercy of God, king of the Franks and Lombards). His imperial coinage consisted of a medallion of Constantine on the one side, and on the reverse was a church with the inscription *Religio Christiana*. The Roman-Christian imperial ideology, the *Imperium Christianum* (Christian Empire) had been re-established once again. The universality of the Church contributed to the consolidation of the Empire, and, conversely, the wide expanse of the Empire made possible a uniform organization of the ecclesiastical domain.

The marriage of Church and Empire was soon to prove troublesome. The Church felt that the temporal rulers were encroaching on ecclesiastical power. The Church, on the one hand, expected imperial protection, but, on the other hand, it claimed recognition as an *altera res publica*, a distinct commonwealth, centered around the Sacraments and the church property and ruled by the bishops, and that it should carry on its own tasks within the framework of canon law. The papacy strongly clung to the conviction that the *Imperium* was at its service. It was the papacy that conferred imperial dignity by the anointing and the coronation, and according to Roman and ecclesiastical tradition, this meant, an act that the Pope freely does and it presupposes the examination of the one to be anointed. Such a claim by the papacy touched the foundations of the autonomy of secular rulers and gave rise to a perennial conflict over the issue of supremacy.

With the disintegration of the Carolingian Empire, Otto I and his successors succeeded in their attempts to bring the papacy and the Church under their subjection. The papal elections were not only subjected to imperial confirmation, as was the case under the Carolingian Lothar I and Louis II, but the German Emperors also participated in the election discussions in an authoritative manner so as to be able even to designate the candidate. Bishoprics and abbeys were more and more incorporated into the political organization of the time, dominated by feudal views of sovereignty and propiretorship.

Throughout this struggle, the Roman Church was able to uphold her claims to political freedom. One of the main reasons was the existence of the Papal State, that remnant of Byzantine rule in Central Italy, which "let the papacy take the place there of the *basileus* and even claim imperial symbols of sovereignty, such as robes of state or tiara and imperial court ceremonial."[18]

The acknowledgement of the pope's spiritual authority as *vicarius Petri* (Vicar of Peter) on the other hand, protected the existence of the Papal State. The Church never gave up its claim for total freedom from dependency and control by temporal rulers, and it finally launched its struggle over the principle of the freedom of the Church with the Gregorian Reform. Rising to the defense of its rights, the Church aimed, in the face of the civil power to vindicate itself as a *societas perfecta,* a "perfect society."[19]

The Era of Gregorian Reform

The issue of lay investiture of bishops brought a head-on conflict between the ecclesiastical and imperial jurisdictions. Pope Gregory VII prohibited lay investiture of bishops in 1075. The following year Emperor Henry IV tried to secure the deposition of Gregory who replied by excommunicating Henry. From Gregory's point of view the pope was the sovereign head of the whole Church. He alone could create and depose bishops; he alone could call general council and give effect to its decrees. Papal decrees, on the other hand, could be annulled by no one and the Pope was subject to no other authority. Gregory's position was a development of the Church's admitted jurisdiction over questions of morals and doctrine. The Church was acknowledged as having spiritual authority to exercise moral discipline over every member of the community. It is not our concern here to determine whether Gregory intended to claim legal supremacy over the secular sphere and ruler. It is clear that his objective was to protect the independence of the Church, by claiming for it final authority in matters of morals and doctrine. The Church looked upon itself as the repository of moral ideals and civic order.

The Gregorian Reform was a turning-point in the self-understanding of the Church. The spirit of Gregorian Reform, present even before Gregory VII, saw that the only possible way to extricate the Church from her subjection to secular powers was to assert the Church as a juridically con-stituted society. Reform, especially for Gregory VII, meant that the Church must seek to make itself a self-governing community. Gregory VII felt that the internal reform depended on the Church extricating herself from subjection to secular powers. His main concern was to assert the rights and jurisdictional powers of the clerical order, or more accurately of the papacy, in the face of secular powers.

The battle for the autonomy of ecclesiastical jurisdiction was fought in the arena of the law. Gregory VII asked canon lawyers to search out and assemble all the texts that could be used to support the autonomy of papal authority and, under it, a wholesome order in the Church. The main concern of the papacy was to assert its rights in the face of resistance and encroachment by secular powers. The issue of empire versus papacy became a legal contest, a contest of rights and powers.[20] The legal battle gave rise to the ascendancy of Canon Law, making it a universal ecclesiastical science, especially with Gratian, the classic exponent of the new law. The Gregorian Reform succeeded in establishing the Church as an entity of its own right, independent and sovereign in its realm.

The conflict between Pope Boniface VIII and Philip the Fair further heightened the claims of sovereignty of power vested in the pope. The bull *Unam Sanctam* (1301) asserted the supreme authority of the pope over the whole Church and the supremacy of the spiritual over temporal power. It said:

> We are taught by the words of the Gospel that in this Church and under its control there are two swords, the spiritual and the temporal....Both of these, that is, the spiritual and the temporal swords, are under the control of the Church. The first is wielded by the Church; the second is wielded on behalf of the Church. The first is wielded by the hand of the priest, the second by the hand of kings and soldiers but at the wish and by the permission of the priests. Sword must be subordinated to sword, and it is only fitting that the temporal authority should be subject to the spiritual.[21]

The position taken by Boniface followed the course taken by the popes of the 13th century, especially Innocent III and Innocent IV. The list of powers which these popes claimed and exercised, supported by the canon lawyers, did not express a rejection of the ancient distinction between the two powers or even the denial that the two were distinct in purpose and in their exercise. However, the supposed independence and separation of *sacerdotium* and *imperium* was in process of being explained away, a process that reached its culmination with Boniface VIII.

On the occasion of this conflict in the space of a few months between 1301-1302, influential treatises appeared on ecclesiology: the *De Regimine Christiano* of James of Viterbo; the *De Ecclesiastica Potestate* of Giles of Rome; the *De Potestate Papali et Regali* of John of Paris and many others. The authors were real theologians, and as their titles suggest, these were treatises on the Church's authority and power dealing with a theology of juridical powers of clerical order. It was a time of a theology of hierarchical power, a theology wherein juridical categories of thought defined ecclesiology.[22] The theologians had embarked on a theory of political society in their attempt to define Church, "they saw the people itself as the body politic, the public service of this body politic appertaining to the highest levels of society, what we call an Estate."[23]

The absolutist claim of the papacy was not a mere academic question. It meant "the tightening up of the whole process of government, including papal control over the giving of benefices, the drawing of ecclesiastical cases into the papal courts, the diversion of great sums of money into the papal revenues, and the systematic exercise of irritating reforms of papal taxation."[24] The whole ecclesiastical organization became infected with corruption and abuses. The Great Schism, which lasted from 1378 to 1417, made matters worse. The Church needed reform.

The Councils of Constance (1414-1418) and Basel (1431-1449) were convoked as instruments of reform within the Church. The advocates of conciliar reform were primarily interested in restoring unity in the Church and in bringing about the necessary reforms in the government of the Church. They were not interested in changing the whole principle of church government by abolishing supremacy of the pope.[25] They defended the supreme importance of the Council for the life of the Church, on the basis that it represents, better than any individual can, the whole Church. The essential principle of the conciliar theory was that the whole body of the Church, the congregation of the faithful, is endowed with spiritual power, and it is a society that possesses all the means and powers needed to insure its perpetuity, its orderly government, and the removal of abuses as they occur. The clergy, including the pope, are organs by which this society acts. The substance of the conciliar theory, was that the Church is a complete and self-sufficing society, in which resides the self-governing power. The clerics, including the pope, and even the councils are organs of the ecclesiastical government.

From the 12th century onwards, within the Church there had been currents reducing Christianity to a spiritual fellowship; these movements are characterized by an anti-institutional and anti-hierarchical attitude. They disregarded the institution of the Church as a necessary order to salvation in Christian economy. Representing this tendency of interiority were the different groups of "Apostolics" who stressed the personal goodness of life, and envisaged faith as purely personal and thus reduced the Church to an assembly of faithful. Then there were the communal movements which belonged to general history; driven as they were by economic, political and cultural factors, these movements rather promoted democratic tendencies.[26] The application of democratic ideas to the self-understanding of the Church was aroused by a conjunction of various political and social events, but a forceful theological articulation was given by Marsiglio of Padua, John of Janduno and William of Ockam. They viewed the Church as the sum of faithful individuals, and the bishops and priests only as representatives of the faithful.[27]

The hierarchy of the Church reacted strongly by accentuating precisely those features that the adversaries were denying. As Congar points out, it re-affirmed essentially "the authority of the Church" as rule of faith, of hierarchical powers, particularly of the papal primacy, and of the visibility of the Church and her members."[28] This conception of things came to be reinforced by developments of later Roman law, those of imperial absolutism. The Roman juridical idea was of a sovereign exercising dominion over a given territory, imposing a uniform system and ruling the life of the whole body.[29] It envisaged society as a given domain over which a sovereign central authority exercised power. A socio-political notion of authority of the Church, was by now in place.

The Reformation Era

The Reformation brought on the most serious crisis with respect to the socio-political self-understanding of the Church. The reformers' notions of a priesthood of all believers and justification by faith alone directly challenged the hierarchical structure. Protestantism rejected the whole of the Church's mediation: the magisterium, the priesthood, the sacraments, and the role of the teaching Church as the rule of faith. The reality of the Church as an institution for salvation was fundamentally disregarded. Although the ecclesial institution was accepted as the order of the means of grace, attention was given only to the final reality of salvation wrought in each faithful soul by an act of God alone.

Against Protestantism, the Council of Trent stressed all the more the aspect of visible hierarchical society, juridically instituted. In opposition to the Protestant theory of the invisible Church and salvation as an inward reality, Catholic apologists pressed the doctrine of her visibility, as an objectively constituted external and juridical machinery of the means of grace and the hierarchical mediation of the means to salvation. They reasserted her authority and gave it a greater degree of centralization, at the same time promoting a "mystique" around authority, by identifying God's will completely with the institutional form of authority. In the latter, it is God's own voice we hear and heed.

Roman Catholic ecclesiology became mainly, sometimes almost exclusively, an affirmation of the Church "as machinery of hierarchical mediation, of the powers and primacy of the Roman see, in a word, a 'hierarchology'."[30] Authority was posited first and foremost as authority for its own sake and as a result it was looked upon in a purely juridical and sociological sense. The Church came to be seen as practically nothing more than a society in which some commanded and the rest obeyed. As Congar rightly remarks, *Ecclesia* came to indicate "not so much the body of the faithful as the system, the apparatus, the impersonal depository of the system of rights whose representatives are the clergy or, as it is now called, the Hierarchy, and ultimately the Pope and the Roman Curia."[31]

The threat of subservience of the Church to the State continued all the more vigorously in the Reformation and post- Reformation era, which political historians call "the age of absolutism." In spite of theoretical administrative control by the Pope, the Roman Church had to accommodate to the circumstances of the national churches.They were held together in doctrine and in communion by their tie with the

Vatican, but in several of the major countries the Pope had little or no voice in the naming of the bishops and his decrees could be circulated or obeyed only with the consent of the Crown.

In Spain, the monarchs were zealous of their control of the Church. Popes granted to the kings of Spain the patronage of all churches and convents in lands conquered from the Moors, and the *real patronato*, the   right of nomination to the benefices in these territories. A similar situation prevailed as far as Portugal was concerned. The crown obtained a large degree of control over the Church. In both the Spanish overseas possessions, and in the Portuguese colonial empire, the crown was given the *padroado* of all benefices.[32] However by means of various Concordats, the Church aimed to safeguard its autonomy and independence.

The Caesaropapist trend manifested itself also in what came to be termed as Gallicanism. Its proponents insisted on liberties that curtailed the authority of the Pope on local churches. In 1682 Louis XIV declared that the King had the right to receive the fees from all vacant sees, and to fill vacant sees as he wishes; that no Papal Legate could exercise his functions in France, without royal permission, that the king could legislate for the Church, and that no Papal bulls could be put in execution without the approval of the king. Although papal protests eventually led to a partial disavowal by Louis XIV,[33] Gallicanist trends persisted in France.

The trend similar to Gallicanism prevailed in Germany under what came to be known as Febronianism, taking its name from the pseudonym, Justinus Febronius, under which Nikolaus von Hontheim, Auxiliary Bishop of Trier, wrote. The Febronian views had a wide support throughout Europe in spite of Rome's continual resistance. In the latter part of the 18th century various monarchs further extended the control of the State over the Church. Outstanding among them was Frederick II the Great, (1712-1786), King of Prussia. He insisted on controlling the Church, whether it was Protestant or Roman Catholic, and reserved the right to appoint ecclesiastics in the Roman Church, from parish priests to bishops. The other prominent figure was Holy Roman Emperor Joseph II (1741 - 1790) who framed a structure of his own for a national church. His religious policy came to be known as Josephism. Besides Austria, his ideas spread in some of the states of Italy where Austria had control. Joseph II dissolved a large number of monasteries, largely those of contemplatives, encouraged monks to become secular priests or even take up secular occupations, replaced diocesan and monastic schools with state institutions, abolished some of the ecclesiastical holidays, compiled cathechisms for the instruction of youth which minimized catholic dogma and stressed morals. He attempted to make clergy entirely dependent on the State for their subsistence.[34] In Italy, which was divided politically, lay princes who ruled over the political entities which were not within the Papal States sought to increase their control of ecclesiastical affairs. The history of Western Europe, especially since the later Middle Ages, is marked by an ongoing tension and conflict between Church and State, the Church struggling to maintain its independence and autonomy in the wake of attempts of State domination.

The Era of Political Revolutions

The great wave of revolution, which broke over Europe in the course of the nineteenth century, led to further institutional consolidation of the Church. The Church was at a loss as to what attitude to adopt to the world born out of the intellectual and political revolution of 1789 and its after-effects, in particular to the new consciousness of civil and religious liberties. In Italy Pius IX, although in deep sympathy with the Italian Cause and independence for Italians from Austrian domination, was not ready to support the unification of Italy under the aegis of anti-clerical Piedmont which advocated the disappearance of the Papal State. Pius IX attached great importance to his temporal sovereignty, for he saw in it the indispensable guarantee of the pope's spiritual independence. His personal misfortunes in the wake of Roman Revolution and its bloody memories convinced him all the more of his personal distrust of liberal principles. He saw a causal link between the principles of 1789 and the destruction of traditional values in the social, moral and religious order. Attacks on the faith, confused ideas about liberty and authority, which menaced the tranquillity of the State and the public order, had become sources of great concern for Pius IX.

The French Catholics were dismayed at the news of the proclamation of the Republic in 1848, since the word conjured up unhappy memories of the outrages against the social and religious order, that characterized the first Republic half a century before. The program of social reforms advanced by the new regime was not understood by the great majority of Catholics, most of whom belonged to rural communities or to the petty bourgeoisie. Their sensitivity to the maintenance of social order and to the intangibility of the "sacred dogma of property" made them panicky and resentful of the revolution. They felt that religion and morality were threatened along with the trad- itional social order. To them and even to some bourgeois circles, the Church presented the sole effective bulwark of the existing social order. Many longed for a Church with a regime of external privileges and prestige along with a strong socio-political structure that had marked the Christianity of the past. They saw the modern world chiefly as anti- Christian, and thus believed that the Church should shore up defenses against it. It was also a fact that every time the liberals came to power, they lost no time in introducing legislation not merely unfavorable to the Church, but even hostile especially on the subject of education and religious orders.

The ultramontane movement reached its apogee during this period. Although the movement had gained momentum during the pontificate of Gregory XVI, it took a strong hold and seal of approval under Pius IX.[35] The fears of direct collision with governments, hostile in principle to greater papal intervention in the affairs of national Churches, led to systematic efforts to rally Catholic forces around Rome and the papacy to battle against "revolutionary and anti-Christtian" liberalism. The ideas of papal primacy and the Church's "indirect power" in civil society were popularized and disseminated throughout the world, and some did not even hesitate to advocate direct power for the Church and the pope over civil society.

There was special effort to consolidate the life within the Church. All the national Churches were exhorted to return to full observance of canon law. Episcopal appointments were made not based on the recommendations sent in by the local clergy, but based on the candidate's personal loyalty to the Roman primate. More and more national seminaries were opened in Rome. Priests who were loyal to the Roman autocracy received all possible encouragement and promotions.   Anything likely to perpetuate regional differences in the life of the Church was frowned upon. The questions of liturgy, discipline and appointments were increasingly decided by the pope and the Curia. Thus the Church in a climate of confusion and external threats attempted to bring about an organic coherence by strengthening the papal authority. Under conditions of organizational failure or crisis, the most typical response is greater institutionalization of the existing power structure. The Church shaped itself into a closed world ruled by a self-sufficient order of its own.

Such a stage of institutional consolidation of the Church was a culmination of a long process. The chaos and the violence of the Revolutions and the ensuing political situations left a wave of anxiety and turmoil in the European population as a whole, and thus many "sought haven in a church which to them appeared to offer security in a world whose foundations were crumbling."[36]

Although the Church came to be portrayed as the embodiment of order, it conceived of itself as nothing less than a divinely established order. Thus the introduction to the constitution *Pastor Aeternus* of Council Vatican I states:

> The eternal Shepherd and Guardian of our souls (see 1 Pet.
> 2:25), in order to render the saving work of redemption
> lasting, decided to establish his holy Church that in it, as
> in the house of the living God, all the faithful might be
> held together by the bond of one faith and one love.... But
> the gates of hell, with a hatred that grows greater each day,
> are rising up everywhere against its divinely established
> foundation with the intention of overthrowing the Church,
> if this were possible.[37]

The self-understanding of the Church as a socio-political
entity had reached its apogee. The whole nature of the
Church came to be understood in terms of a visible and
perfect society to be governed under a system of
supernatural order. It could be argued that even the
definition of infallibility was first a statement about the
socio-political structure of the Church and secondarily a
theological doctrine, as the very preamble of the definition
seems to suggest:

> But since in this present age, which especially requires the
> salutary efficacy of the apostolic office, not a few are
> found who minimize its authority, We think it extremely
> necessary to assert solemnly the prerogative which the
> only begotten Son of God deigned to join to the highest
> pastoral office.[38]

It seems obvious that the socio-political self-
understanding of the Church developed in response to
historical realities. It was shaped not only by its assimilation
and integration with the surrounding environment, but also
as a result of its organizational response to real or perceived
threats.

In any field we take a good look at ourselves when we
are criticized; it is within the context of threatening situations
that we strive to define ourselves. And so, the
ecclesiological problems raised by m en and events led the
Church to define itself. In face of the civil power, the

Church vindicated itself as a "perfect society," a juridically constituted self-sufficing entity that possesses all the means and powers to attain its end. In the face of Protestantism, it attempted to vindicate itself as a visible hierarchical society, and its authority as rule of faith. While the Reformers were reducing the Church to an inward Christianity, to salvation, Catholic apologists presented the Church as the machinery of the means of grace, as the hierarchical mediation of the means to salvation. Thus the Church for Roman Christianity came to indicate more of a system, a system of doctrines and sacramental institutions, a code of morality and discipline and a comprehensive penal system, all founded upon a power of jurisdiction, presumed to be entrusted by Christ; that the Christian religion could not be practiced except in and through the system of this "*societas perfecta*," and that outside this society there can be no true religion of Christ.[39]

2. CHURCH AS A BODY POLITIC

From the time Christianity became the official religion of the Roman Empire, the prevailing view among the early Fathers like Ambrose, Augustine and Gregory the Great was that the entire human society was divinely ordained to be ruled by two orders. Spiritual interests and eternal salvation were in the keeping of the clerical order; temporal interests were in the keeping of the civil government. Mankind formed a single society under two jurisdictions, each with its own law, its own organs of government and its own rights. Between these two orders, a spirit of mutual helpfulness was to prevail. However, this view, known as the doctrine of two swords, never became a viable doctrine in actuality. For the next millenium the ecclesiastical and civil jurisdictions were engaged in a constant struggle for supremacy and control of one by the other. The spiritual and the temporal were regarded as two arms of one body, a single *societas christiana* (christian society). The question of right relationship of powers became the prime consideration of the age as well as the crux of the conflict. The Church in its struggle to defend her freedom from control by temporal rulers, sought to make herself a self-governing community, an entity in her own right, independent and sovereign in her realm.

The term *societas christiana* gradually came to denote the body of the baptized faithful, embracing both the clergy and laity, and this body was the "*Ecclesia*": *omnes fideles tam laici quam clerici sunt membra Ecclesiae*[40] (all the faithful, lay as well as clerics are members of the Church). *Ecclesia* in other words stood for the corporate union of the whole Christian people into one body. It is not of interest to this study to detail the historical and ideological factors responsible to this idea. One may observe, however, that the corporational notion became integral to the understanding of the Church as a juridical entity.

This corporate body of Christians is at the same time a civil society, a universal body politic. The universalism of this society should not be seen as territorial but rather covering every aspect of social, cultural and political life. The purpose of this Christian society was to pursue the ideal ways of life, the divinely imposed order; for all the Middle Ages looked back to a Golden Age when the right universal order had been laid down by God.[41]   The *Ecclesia* envisioned itself as embodying that universal divine order and the universal mode of right living.   Therefore the *Ecclesia* was considered not merely an aggregate of the persons who composed it, but also a mystical entity that existed over and above the members. It is an entity existing outside the world of particulars and is best described as a "universal." It is this "universal" which is the essence of *Ecclesia*, that is infinitely more important than any of its particular members, and exists over and above them; it is on a level with the "*species*" and "*genera*" which alone have true reality. This mysterious essence of *Ecclesia*, like Plato's Ideal lies in the heavenly realm[42] and embodies a divine pattern of existence; in the final analysis it is identical *with* the heavenly Christ Himself. The *Ecclesia* as a societal organization, therefore, is the structure in which the Christian essence of goodness assumes a visible nature. Within such an understanding, *Ecclesia* stands, on the one hand, for the corporate union of the whole Christian people, and on the other hand, it is infinitely more than any of its members, as it exists over and above them.

When the above conception is put into legal phraseology, the *Ecclesia* is immediately recognizable as a corporation. By the Roman law theory of corporations, the juridical person of the Roman *respublica* becomes the mystical person of the Christian society, existing in a heavenly, spiritual realm and to be identified with heavenly Christ Himself.[43] In order to convey and consolidate the idea of the Church as a body with an essence that transcended its members, the expression *Corpus Mysticum* was gradually attributed to the Ecclesia and finally became its official designation. Thus a real "mystique" was created around the ecclesiastical institution, as an embodiment of a theonomy (a divine law). And as Yves Congar rightly remarks, the strength of any movement lies in its "mystique."[44]

Since this corporate body of Christians is a universal body politic, it requires a government as a controlling and unifying principle. The political theory of Aristotle was amalgamated with the Christian view of human being in the understanding of the Church as a society, especially from St. Thomas onwards.[45] The civil society (State) is for St. Thomas, as for Aristotle, a natural institution, founded on the nature of human being. Human being, like every creature, has its own end, but it is not an isolated entity which can attain its end simply as an individual. A human person is by nature a social or political being, born to live in community with its fellow beings, therefore society is natural to humans. Thus, the State is a "perfect society" (*societas perfecta*), i.e. it has at its disposal all the means necessary for the attainment of its end, the *bonum commune,* the common good of the citizens. In its struggle for autonomy and independence from the State and within the context of apologetic, the Church appropriated the notion of a "perfect society," as a self-sufficing entity having all the means necessary to attain its end. Although the end of the Church is supernatural, but because it is a society, it needs a government as a controlling and unifying principle.

Since the *Ecclesia* expresses a divine pattern of right living, those who govern the Christian people were regarded as having the function to translate that pattern into positive laws. The constitutive element of this society is not racial or national or biological, but the supernatural element of the Christian faith. Although all those who have accepted the doctrines of Christianity and have been baptized form this body, this body is made up of two orders, *ordo clericalis* and *ordo laicalis*. The members of the *ordo clericalis* alone are qualified to function as the directing and governing organs of this society, for they alone are functionally qualified to direct society according to its underlying purpose. Although baptism might be enough to secure membership in the society, it does not give each member the right to participate in its government. Through ordination the members of the sacerdotal order are given the power to bind and to loose, to sanctify and to teach the Christian faith, thus making them functionally qualified to govern the Christian society, which is genetically and substantially a spiritual society.[46] This functionalist approach is based on the teleological principle which was a living force in the medieval period. In the great world machine, each person was considered to have his own proper place with his rights and duties. One belonged to a certain order that was part of an overall hierarchical system. By fulfilling the functions attached to each individual order, there would emerge *harmonia et pax* (harmony and peace) and the society would fulfill the purpose for which it existed.[47]

Furthermore, the governing authority came to be regarded not merely as a directing force to the entire ecclesiastical society, but also the embodiment of the juridical personality of the ecclesiastical corporation. This connotation was widely used by the defenders of papal absolutism. There was a legal fiction which distinguished the body taken as a single corporate whole from members individually, and while the corporate whole is permanent, having the status of *persona juridica* (juridical personality), the individuals that make that corporate whole are transitory and do pass away. Papacy as an office came to be regarded as the ultimate embodiment of the juridical personality of the entire body. For papalists, what the pope does was what the corporate body of Christians can be said to do. Hence, authority became the formal element of the Church. The ecclesiology, especially from the post-Reformation period, "became fixed in a set pattern in which the question of authority is so predominant that the whole treatise is more like a hierarchology."[48] The fundamental self-understanding of the Church became that of a socio-juridical entity (in which some command and the rest obey), a universal body politic. By the nineteenth century, the official ecclesiastical documents widely refer to the Church as "ecclesiastical society," "religious society," "Christian society" in contrast to the "civil society" (v.g. *Singulari Quidem*, March 17,

1856; *Cum Nuper,* Jan. 20, 1858.), "catholic (sacred or christian) commonwealth" in contrast to the "civil commonwealth" (v.g. *Qui Pluribus*, Nov. 9, 1846; *Ubi Primum*, June 17,1847; *Nostis et Nobiscum*, Dec. 8, 1849; *Ubi Nos*, May 15, 1871). The *Syllabus Errorum* issued by Pius IX (Dec. 8, 1864) declared it to be an error to hold that "the Church is not a true, and perfect, and entirely free society."[49]

The self-understanding that the Church claimed and established for itself was of a reactive nature. As Congar rightly remarks, the Church ended up being understood as "nothing more than a society in which some commanded and the rest obeyed; but above all it exalted the place of those in authority. It considered the Church from the viewpoint of her rights and the powers that made her a social structure; in a word, as a juridical subject of authority and rights."[50] The socio-political self-understanding of the 19th century Church was a result of appropriation by the Church of the reality behind the political theory of "perfect society" and the Roman Law corporation theory of "juridical personality."

3. AUTHORITY AS A POWER TO RULE

For a Church whose nature was that of a body politic, the place of a ruling authority became central to its mission. This section calls attention specifically to the fact that within a socio-political self-understanding, authority in the Church came to amount to the right to command obedience, a relationship of superior to inferior, a *dominium* (dominion) of clerical elite over the rest.

With the Gregorian Reform, the self-understanding of the Church as a monarchic republic constituted and ordained for the purpose of attaining the supernatural salvation of souls, became established. The pope under God and the divine law was its ruler, as lawful successor of Peter. In virtue of his succession the pope was the vicar of Christ, and as vicar he had received from him authority to rule and to teach *(principatum et magisterium)* over all Churches, over all the clerics and faithful. In the mind of Gregory VII, while the succeeding popes might be "inferior to Peter in sanctity and in the power of working miracles, they are in every respect his equals so far as their jurisdiction is concerned."[51] By this time, a new element had been strongly integrated into ecclesiology, the legal science. Canon law became of paramount importance during the struggle of the priesthood, or more accurately of the papacy, to assert its rights in the face of the secular power.[52]

Authority in the Church came to be identified with the ecclesiastical jurisdiction, allegedly instituted by Christ. This jurisdictional authority came to be regarded as the very foundation of the Church. The dominant ideal underlying the ecclesiastical authority was that a ruling "power" was given at the beginning by Christ, to his "vicar," that is, to a representative who takes his place, and who hands on that power to those who come after him in historical sequence of transmission and succession. The transworldly or heavenly power, which initially in a "vertical" descent was given to the earthly representative, then by means of "horizontal" transmission passes on to the successors. Supported by a legal structure, authority in the Church was given a formal validity.

Unfortunately, this development led to the understanding of authority in the Church solely from a legalistic perspective, its validity linked to a title in law. The theology of authority in the Church became attached to the formal and juridical elements, totally devoid of any link to Christian perfection or reality of grace. Furthermore many of the features of the imperial court were borrowed, like vocabulary, insignia, ceremonial, ideology and style. Power invited symbols of power.The Church defended its autonomous juridical power as divinely established, and in fact this perspective became paradigmatic in its self - understanding.

Official documents consistently evision authority in terms of power of jurisdiction. For instance, the Second Council of Lyons (1274), was concerned with reuniting the Greek Church which was in schism with the Roman Church. The creed to which the emperor of the East Michael Paleologus subscribed, contained, besides the issue of the famous *Filioque*, an acknowledgement of the supreme jurisdictional power of the Roman Church. It stated:

> The same holy Roman Church also has supreme and full primacy and jurisdiction over the whole Catholic Church. This is truly and humbly recognized as received from the Lord himself in the person of St. Peter, the Prince or the head of the Apostles, whose successor in the fullness of power is the Roman Pontiff.[53]

In the controversy between Boniface VIII and Philip the Fair, the position of papal imperialism reached its heights. The bull *Unam Sanctam* (1302) took the most advanced ground on papal jurisdictional supremacy that was ever written into an official document.[54] It asserted the supreme authority of the Pope over the whole Church and the supremacy of the spiritual over temporal power.

The Council of Florence (1438-45), in its Decree for the Greeks, reiterated the idea of the fullness of juridical power given to the supreme head of the Roman Church. It stated:

> Likewise, we define that the holy Apostolic See and the Roman Pontiff is the successor of St. Peter, the Prince of the Apostles, ad the true vicar of Christ, the head of the whole Church, the father and teacher of all Christians; and that to him, in the person of St. Peter, was given by our Lord Jesus Christ the full power of feeding, ruling, and governing the whole Church.[55]

The Reformation questioned authority not only in its historical forms, but as a principle. It refused the right of any human authority to enter into the field of man's relationship with God. It rejected the rights of the juridical authority of the institutional Church to rule the spiritual realm of humans. The Church in its turn defended its institutional system and reiterated that its juridical authority was the rule of faith. Congar notes that scholastic ecclesiology by the end of the sixteenth century "was hardly more than the apologetic version of a treatise on public ecclesiastical law; it was entirely preoccupied with powers and rights."[56]

After the French Revolution, the doctrine of divinely established juridical authority was exploited with an exclusive emphasis on papal powers. A Letter of the Holy Office written to the Bishops of England in September of 1864 states:

> The true Church of Jesus Christ is constituted by divine authority and is known by four notes. We lay down these notes as matters of faith in the Creed. And any one of these notes is so joined to the others that it cannot be separated from them. Hence it is that the Church that really is catholic, and is called Catholic, must, at the same time, shine with the prerogatives of unity, sanctity, and apostolic succession. Therefore, the Catholic Church is

> one by a conspicuous and perfect unity of the whole world
> and of all peoples, by that unity, indeed, whose principle,
> root, and never-failing source is in the supreme authority
> and "greater sovereignty" of St .Peter, the Prince of the
> Apostles, and of his successors in the Roman Chair.[57]

In his encyclical *Quanta Cura* of December 8, 1864, Pius IX reaffirmed the independence of the sacred from secular juridical power, alleging that the former was established by Christ himself. He stated that "Christ our Lord with his divine authority gave to the Roman Pontiff the supreme power of shepherding, ruling and governing the Church."[58]

Vatican Council I gave a definitive seal to the socio-political self-understanding of the Church in its papal apex, and above all to its understanding of authority as power of jurisdiction. The first Draft of the Dogmatic Constitution stated:

> Christ's Church is not a society of equals as if all the
> faithful in it had the same rights; but is a society in which
> not all are equal. And this is so not only because some of
> the faithful are clerics and some laymen, but especially
> because in the Church there is a power of divine
> institution, by which some are authorized to sanctify,
> teach and govern, and others do not have this authority.
> Since, however, there is a twofold power in the Church,
> one called the power of orders and the other called the
> power of jurisdiction, we teach with regard to this latter
> power in particular that it is jurisdiction that is absolute
> and perfectly complete, legislative, judicial, and coercive,
> and that it pertains not only to the internal and sacramental
> forum but also to the external and public. The subjects of
> this power are the pastors and teachers appointed by
> Christ.[59]

In its final text of the Dogmatic Constitution on the Church, Vatican I declared:

> We teach and declare, therefore, according to the testimony

of the Gospel that the primacy of jurisdiction over the whole Church of God was immediately and directly promised to and conferred upon the blessed Apostle Peter by Christ the Lord.... After his Resurrection, Jesus conferred upon Simon Peter alone the jurisdiction of supreme shepherd and ruler over his whole fold with the words, "Feed my lambs....Feed my sheep" (John 21:15-17).[60]

And the Canon declared:

Therefore, if anyone says that the blessed Apostle Peter was not constituted by Christ the Lord as the Prince of all the Apostles..., or that he received immediately and directly from Jesus Christ our Lord only a primacy of honor and not a true and proper primacy of jurisdiction: let him be anathema.[61]

Elucidating the nature of the primacy it stated:

We teach and declare that,...this power of jurisdiction of the Roman Pontiff,... is immediate. Regarding this jurisdiction, the sheperds of whatever rite and dignity and the faithful, individually and collectively, are bound by a duty of hierarchical subjection and of sincere obedience.[62]

And the Canon declared:

If anyone says that the Roman pontiff has only the office of inspection or direction, but not the full and supreme power of jurisdiction over the whole Church, not only in matters that pertain to faith and morals, but also in matters that pertain to the discipline and government of the Church throughout the world; or if anyone says that he has only a more important part and not the complete fullness of this supreme power; or if anyone says that this power is not ordinary and immediate either over each and every church or over each and every shepherd and faithful memeber: let him be anathema.[63]

Although this study is not specifically dealing with the papacy, what we need to observe is that authority in the Church came to be confined solely to the power of jurisdiction. Everything else, including the reality of grace and Spirit, was accommodated to suit the juridical reality. As Congar would remark; "We see living spiritual reality, inner quality and personal involvement degraded into *things*."[64]

The term "jurisdiction" comes from "*Juris*" and "*dico*" meaning "I speak by the law." The *Oxford Dictionary* defines jurisdiction as the power of declaring and administering law or justice." The standard definition in legal science is: *Jurisdictio est potesta de publico introducta cum necessitate juris dicendi* (jurisdiction is a power introduced for the public good, on account of the necessity of dispensing justice).[65] Jurisdictional power is inextricably linked to law or justice to be dispensed.

The ecclesiastical jurisdiction claimed to dispense *divina justitia* (divine justice). The *societas christiana* (christian society) was to be ruled under a divine universal order, a theonomy, termed also *justitia* .[66]

The concept of *justitia* contained the totality of all principles that make up the divine order, or the supreme canon of the Christian world order. The task of the jurisdictional authority was to translate the eternal order into positive requirements; it had to give divine righteousness a concrete form to be adopted by mankind, it had to define the universal canon of right order into concrete precepts. And the articulation of the universal divine order was to be done by means of law. All the different modalities of law, like the *statuta*, the *decreta*, the *dicta*, the *regulae*, the *sanctiones*, the *canones*, (the stautes, the decrees, the pronouncements, the rules, the sactions, the canons), were expressions of the divinely established right order. The Christian gospel itself came to be epitomized in the idea of law, observes Walter Ullman.[67] The substance of *justitia* was the right norm of living and believing, that which stood for the right conduct appropriate to the Christian society and which would finally lead the members to eternal salvation.

Finally, the governing of the Christian society was to be

done only by the ordained members. They alone were uniquely qualified to be the directing and governing organs because they were functionally qualified to lay down the *norma justitiae*.[68] Through ordination, members of the clerical order were regarded as given the power to bind and loose, giving them functional qualification to rule the Christian society. The *sacerdotium* (priesthood) was the vehicle by which *justitia* was articulated and enforced in the *societas christiana*.

The general term used to denote the ecclesiastical authority was *sacra potestas* or "sacred" power, in contrast to the "temporal" power of the secular ruler. The concept of sacred or spiritual power stood for the ruling power needed to ordain spiritual interests, the interests of the soul for the purpose of attaining its eternal salvation; while the temporal power was ordained toward the material interests or the interests of the body. Like the temporal, the spiritual power was equally conceived as *dominium* of the clerical order over the laity. Since the Church was a *societas christiana*, its governing organ had the responsibility to direct its members to their heavenly end by translating and enforcing the *divina justitia* by means of doctrines and laws. Such an authority may be characterized as follows: 1) it signified a *dominium* of the ruler over the ruled; 2) it meant a legal title for an office; the power was possessed by virtue of an office.

4. Summary Remarks

By affirming that the self-understanding of the Roman Catholic Church bcame socio-political, I do not intend to imply that among the faithful, there was no awareness of being a faith-community called for a life of fellowship under the Fatherhood of God, and for a life of eternal communion with God. Neither do I deny other finer aspects of spiritual life that nourished the life of the Roman Catholic Christians. However, for the official magisterium and for the neo-sholastic theology, the starting point for the understanding of the Church was that of an institutional organization, a socio-juridical entity that had been entrusted with a deposit of eternal truths that lead to salvation. Within such an understanding, authority as a ruling power, became the formal element. For a church whose nature was that of a body politic, ruling power was regarded as central to its mission. It is a fact that in a large number of modern documents, the word "church" indicates the priestly government or even quite simply this government's Roman courts. The place and role of ruling authority became so central, that it came to be regarded as embodying the whole Church.

This socio-juridical self-understanding was a culmination of a long historical process marked by a climate of strife, during which the Church appropriated the realities behind political cncepts and those of Roman Law. It envisioned itself as a concrete historical society, and difined itself primarily as a self-suffcing juridical entity.

The neo-sholastic theology aimed to demonstrate and defend an objective order of divine facts and teachings whose evidence was believed to be open in principle to verification by any right-minded person. That Christian God was an incarnational God, a God not only using history for self-revelation but also giving shape to history. That God's self-revelation came in a final and definitive manner in the person of Jesus of Nazareth and through him God gave a new dispensation, the Church for the salvation of human beings.

Neo-scholasticism presented the Church now as that objective divine order at work. That Church, like Christ, was the visible organ of Divinity because it was a visible continuation of the Incarnate God, Christ himself. Therefore it had qualities like Christ; it was one as Christ was one; it was holy as Christ was holy; it was indefectible as Christ was indefectible; it was infallible as Christ was infallible. The identification of the Church with Christ and finally with the Divinity itself, inevitabley led to the glorification of the Church. The Church was presented as a definitive entity; its institutions and constitution as indefectible and of a divine nature. Such an absolutist self-understanding led the Church to boast before the world of its power, to make claims with regard to God through its decisions, measures and ideas; to suppose that of its own accord, it bestows grace and offers salvation. The Church came to be identified with a fixed order, imposed from above, to which each individual had to submit to, in order to attain eternal salvation.

Finally, the divine order had been entrusted to the care of the sacerdotal organ which ruled the Christian community in accordance with the revealed order. Therefore, urging the faithful to see God in the governing officers of the Church, and God's will in their commands has been a venerable tradition within the Roman Catholic Church. The latter is found rooted in the idea that the ruling power was established by God and bestowed upon a chosen few to rule the Christian Community.

SECTION II:
THEOLOGICAL REFLECTIONS

To explain authority in a juridicial manner, and to confine it to juridicial reality is not only myopic, but a distortion of the true nature of Christian authority.

In this section, I will briefly critique the traditional autocratic notion of authority, as well as the contemporary democratic notion as an ideal, for the authority in the Church.

I will then discuss the Christian Economy (Oikonomia) of God's self-giving in spirit and grace and its implications to the life of the faithful. I suggest that we make Christian Economy the vision and the context, to develop an understanding of authority, which will be of "theological" and not of political nature.

1. A CRITIQUE OF THE TRADITIONAL VIEW

As observed earlier in the historical survey, all kinds of ruling authority, including political authority were unanimously considered to be derived from God.

As for the Church, the sacred "ruling" power was claimed to be established and bestowed by Christ himself on his successors to govern his Church, and therefore God's ruling power was active in his earthly representatives. The perception of ruling power coming down from God can be traced to the pagan concept of Cosmic Divine Government.

In view of the Cosmic Divine Government, the earthly order came to be regarded as a continuation of the transcendent cosmic order. It posited a continuity between the supra-empirical and the empirical, between the heavenly order and the earthly order.

Consequently, the hierarchies of the institutions such as Church and Empire came to be looked upon as custodians and interpreters of the divine cosmic order.[1]

Within this cosmic view, while there was on the one hand, the acknowledgement of the contrast between the profane reality of the world and the sacred, on the other hand, there was the insistence on continuity between the sacred and the profane. The irruption of the sacred into the profane was founded upon the assumption of a continuity and a "communication between the cosmic planes (between earth and heaven)".2

Referring specifically to Christianity in Europe, Eliade writes:

> It is true that most of the rural European populations have been Christianized for over a thousand years. But they succeeded in incorporating into their Christianity a considerable part of their pre-Christian religious heritage, which was of immemorial antiquity.... We may speak of primordial, ahistorical Christianity; by becoming Christians, the European cultivators incorporated into their new faith the cosmic religion that they had preserved from prehistoric times.3

Hence, the Christian tradition, while on the one hand, defended the total transcendence of God, on the other hand, it appropriated the cosmic world-view of pre-Chriatian Era.

Even Thomas Aquinas for instance, in his *Summa* has an entire treatise on the divine government.4 For Thomas all of creation is under the divine government. He writes: "As there can be nothing which is not created by God, so there can be nothing which is not subject to His government."5 Furthermore, "nothing happens outside the order of the Divine Government. No effect results outside the order of the universal cause.... Therefore, as God is the first universal cause, not of one *genus* only, but of all being in general, it is impossible for anything to occur outside the order of the Divine Government."6

An almost paradigmatic trait of all classical Catholic ecclesiology has been, to show a decisive link between the world of God and the world of humans, by claiming that the institutional Church stands for the very divine order, in this world.

This claim gave the institution a semblance of inevitability, permanence and atemporality, lifting it thereby above human and historical contingencies. The Church was presented as existing in the world, but at the same time as transcending this world, because it was a continuation of the heavenly and eternal order. It transcended the individuals and their dificiencies. Standing for a supra-terrestial order, it was purported to speak for God. This notion has been also at the root of triumphalism of the Church.

The supra-human status of the institution of the Church permitted those in governance, to have an ultimate sense of rightness, a sense of authority of supra-human character. Like the institution itself, the governing roles became endowed with a quality of divinity itself. Those who were in governance ruled on behalf of God. The ruling ecclesiastical authority was identified with the absolute standard of God's own governing authority.

When any empirical order is identified in any way with the transcendent reality of God, we fall victim to sacralization. To sacralize natural forces or elements of empirical order is not only inimical to modern science, but it also amounts to the denial of the transcendent God of Christian faith. From a theological perspective, it entails idolatry. And as Charles Davis rightly observes: "Christianity introduced, and doctrinally requires, a radical distinction between the two realms."[7]

Sacralization, on the one hand, assails God's transcendence and ultimacy; and on the other hand, it denies human finitude and creatureliness and instead attempts to make gods out of creatures, raising creatures to the level of God. In the course of its tumultuous history, the Church ended up protecting and defending its institutional self-interests by means of a powerful sacralization.

When anything of the created order, be it a person or an idea or an institution, is raised to the order of the absolute, we fall into idolatry. To elevate any finite reality to be the ultimate measure, or for a human order to make a claim for absolute truth and ultimate reality, is idolatrous.

Christian faith needs to disengage itself from the trappings of a past sacral culture, by upholding the utter transcendence of God. In virtue of that transcendence, God cannot be assigned a place in the universe. God as causality cannot be placed within the cosmic system; neither can God be reduced to a particular function, or to a factor alongside other factors within a cosmic scheme.[8] Furthermore, the transcendent reality is not a mythical realm of eternal ideas, abstract order, or universal reason. In Christian economy, the transcendent reality is a personal God who communes with humans in self-gift.

The central Christian fact consists in God's self-giving realized in the person of Jesus Christ. In virtue of it, human beings have been given the capacity to respond to a self-giving God, to a God who wants to commune with them. This is, what is known as, the order of grace. The transcendent God communicates with humans not through a cosmic order, but through the order of grace.

If there is anything divine within or about humans, it is, as a result of God's self-giving in grace. Therefore, any authority of divine origin has to be understood within the order of grace. A sacralized notion of authority, militates against a true "spiritual", grace-defined concept of authority.

However the temptation to elevate elements of the created order to the level of the divine, to absolutize the finite, remains constant in the Church. As Gregory Baum observes: "Religion remains forever vulnerable to idolatrous trends."[9] It could be further stated that the tendency in human beings to build idols out of the self or creatures, by raising them to a supra-human status, is part of human sinfulness, and hence, the reason why the prophetic warnings against idolatrous trends, were at the core of biblical teaching. Christianity accepts a link between the transcendent God and the order of nature, but it refuses to identify them. And the link is that of grace.

2. THE DEMOCRATIC IDEAL

It is often argued that for the Church to remain relevant to modernity, it needs to reinterpret its authority democratically. That a democratic form has come to stay and that any other conception of authority is simply unthinkable, for the contemporary person.

The term "democracy" is difficult to pin down. Today it has come to be a universally accepted honorific term, although it has undergone a verbal stretching and has become the loosest label of its kind. The term *demokratia* was first used in reference to a system of government practiced in Athens. The system operated as a "town meeting" in which citizens expressed their will and then chose officials to execute the decisions and to demand compliance from all concerned. Hence Greek democracy was based on the actual participation of the citizens in their government.[10]

Etymologically, the term democracy derives from *demos* which means "people" and *kratos*, which means "power". From a normative standpoint the definition of democracy strictly derives from the literal meaning of the term, "power of the people." Hence, something is considered legitimate only when it is derived from the authority of the people and based upon their consent. Originally democracy was used only as a political concept, but in the course of its history it has acquired an ethical significance also.[11] It points to an ideal, it stands for "the ought;" briefly, it does not so much describe a thing, it pre-scribes an ideal. The traditional classicist view defended an autocratic notion of authority in the Church by regarding the priesthood as a ruling class, an "ecclesiastical aristocracy" ruling the entire community of the faithful. A democratic view, in turn, would uphold the primacy of the people of God, and regard authority as being vested in and derived from the people.

But the question is: whether it is theologically justified to hold that the ideal notion of authority in the Church is democratic? Can it be argued that the Church, by its nature, calls for a democratic form of authority?

The democratic view manifests faith in humanity and looks upon the growing democratic spirit as synonymous with progress, and even justifies democrartic ideals as of divine character. In the question of the right relationship between human ideals and the divine, we should caution against making syntheses and identifications. Christian faith, no doubt, is concerned with what is wholesome and ideal, with what is regarded as a true, happy and good human state for the society and the individual. In fact, the dream, the vision or promise of a better society, a fuller life for humanity, forms an essential part of the Christian gospel.[12] Christian faith is intimately connected with an ethos of humanity. However, this does not point to a reduction of Christian faith to the ideal human.

It is true that the concept of democracy has come to indicate not merely a political reality, but also a set of ethical and humanist ideals. A believer is right to interpret any sociopolitical praxis from the perspective of faith, but he or she has to avoid the temptations of sacralizing or supernaturalizing the human reality. The latter can only symbolize and reflect the transcendent reality.

The vision of a fuller life for humanity and the pursuit of the self-realization of human freedom is the essential part of the Kingdom of God on earth, but the Kingdom of God cannot be considered simply identical with human ideals.

The gospel has a prophetic role to play in the history of humanity, and no matter how noble human ideals are, humanity continues to be permeated with greed, selfishness and sinfullnes. Our sense of optimism about the socio-political processes of our time may tempt us to embrace the political concepts indiscriminately. Political theory and practice in the West has come a long way from the political views that were prevalent in the Middle Ages. But, "to notice this evolution is not to imply that democracy is the best political form or that it is terminal; evolution is not synonymous with progress," writes John Mckenzie.[13] Thus, if we believe that the contemporary concept of authority in the Church should be redefined in order to harmonize it with the democratic political theory, then we commit the same kind of mistake, committed by classicist theology. Much as the classicist position upheld and justified the political ideals of a monarchical form within the Church, a democratic vision attempts to uphold and justify the political ideals of a democratic form. Both of these positions fall prey to the temptation of conceiving the Church after the likeness of the State. Furthermore, a theology of authority that merely attempts to replace one type of structure of ruling with another type, does not do justice to the theological concept of authority in the Church, which needs to be understood as singular and *sui generis*.

Secondly, we err in wanting to equate or falsely identify the spiritual reality of "people of God" with the political reality of people, the *demos* understood politically. One reason is, that the nature of authority that the people of God embody, is of a totally different kind than the authority vested in "demos" of a political society. Second, the spiritual authority that resides in the people of God is not something they possess automatically. As much as the people of God have been given the capacity to become the channels of the Spirit of God, it is up to the individual believer to respond to the Spirit and thereby become an efficient channel of grace. On the other hand, in a democratic polis, power is regarded as an inherent right of every member. Hence, an identification of the people of God with the political *demos,* is erroneous.

John Mckenzie, referring to the concept of authority, notes that authority in the Church is neither absolute, nor democratic, but unique in character. It is explicitly different from the known idea of authority in other organizations, because it cannot be discovered by a purely rational analysis. Since the Church is a mystery, its authority shares in the mysterious reality of the Church.[14] Charles Davis, commenting on authority, says: "In itself authority within the Church is *sui generis*; strictly speaking, it is not monarchical nor oligarchical nor democratic."[15] The Church indeed is not a man-made organization, but a community that evolved from the outpouring of God's own Spirit in Christ. It is one thing to stress the communitarian aspect of the Church, but it is a mistake to try to identify the faith community with the political reality of *demos*. However if the concept "democratic" is used analogously, to point out that the common and essential denominator of the Church is the reality of God's Spirit and grace given to all the faithful, and if authority is regarded as a derivative of the grace and the inherent Spirit of God, then one may equate *demos* with the people of God, the Christian *demos*, as the *locus* and substratum of authority.

3. THE CHRISTIAN ECONOMY

According to the Christian faith, as much as God is the mystery *par excellence*, God did not remain inaccessible to human beings. God has communicated to us. This is the chief burden of the Christian message. The human being is not merely made to live in a creator-creature relationship with God, but is called to a more intimate personal relationship. The Christian fact is God's self-giving as it comes to humans. Christian revelation is the self-disclosure made by God to us by means of a personal communion.[16] Or as Karl Rahner expresses it:

> "God wishes to communicate himself, to pour forth the love which he himself is. That is the first and the last of his real plans and hence of his real world too. Everything else exists so that this one thing might be: the eternal miracle of infinite Love. And so God makes a creature whom he can love: he creates man. He creates him in such a way that he *can* receive this Love which is God himself.[17]

It is within the context of this Divine Economy, the economy of God's presence to us, that we have to reflect on how God can be the source of true authority in the community of the faithful.

From a general perspective, theologians following St. Thomas have distinguished three ways in which God may be with the creation.[18] Each of the three modes of presence constitutes a particular manner in which God is present to humankind.

The first mode of God's presence is that by which God is the origin of everything. Things require God's creative power if they are to exist at all. To say that God is Creator is to affirm a relation of total dependence of everything upon God; but this does not affect the internal structure and laws within the universe itself. God cannot be assigned a place within the universe, nor can God's causality be reduced to a particular function within the general scheme. God is everywhere as the ultimate ground of everything. God's causality which gives existence to everything, is God's Being, who is present to the cosmos by the creative power. Briefly, God is present not in a personal way, if we may use the expression, but is present in virtue of the creative power.[19]

The second mode is presence by grace. We are given the power of possessing God as the content of our knowledge and love. We are able to enter into contact with God by the life of faith and love given to us through grace. We can become spiritual temples in the sense that God is able to dwell in us, not merely through the divine power and causality, but according to divine substance and, if we may say so, personally. It is no longer a *presence* of a Creator to the creature, that is involved, but an *indwelling* of a personal God in the faithful. This second mode of presence can only be understood in view of the third mode of God's presence, which is the cause as well as the fulfillment of the former.[20]

The third mode of God's presence was by hypostatic union, through the mystery of Incarnation. In Jesus Christ, God's indwelling is total, ontological. While in grace God unites according to substance, in the Incarnation, God's union to a man was according to the very being. God could not have had a dwelling more intimate and perfect than this. Christ is the decisive reality in and through whom the union of love which God willed for all humans, was fully achieved.

The first two modes of presence were possible, in virtue and in view of God's self-presence in Christ. Finally, through Christ, the messianic gift of the Spirit of God was bestowed upon believers, making thereby each believer and all believers as a body, the sanctuary of God's presence.

According to the Scriptures, the Holy Spirit is the final term of the communication of life from the Father, and the basis of God's innermost communion with human beings. The Holy Spirit is spoken of as dwelling in us, the believers, as in a temple (1 Cor. 3:16; 4:1). Each believer and all believers as a body--the two aspects closely connected--are regarded as the temple of God's presence. All believers as persons are a temple of God's presence. Yet several believers are not several temples, for, one Spirit of God dwells in and sanctifies them all. The faithful all together form one unique and holy temple of God's presence (1 Cor. 3:10-17, 2 Cor. 6:16-18, Eph. 2:14-22).

According to Paul, with the dawn of the messianic era, God has brought to fruition the plan to make the human race a living spiritual temple of self-presence, in which God not only dwells but enters into personal communion with humanity. Hence, the story of God's relationship with creation, and especially with humanity is none other than the story of God's ever more generous, ever deeper presence among the humans. By giving us one's own Spirit, God not only gave us divine gifts--God gave us God's own self.

The Church is therefore the place of God's special presence on earth. Just as God was once thought of as dwelling in a stone temple, God now lives in the community of Christ. The Spirit dwells in it, and is at its foundation. The fact that the Church, the community, is a temple of God's Spirit, implies a charge and a demand upon the members of the community to be worthy temples of the Spirit; since they have been given a spiritual principle, they must lead spiritual lives. Because we are the living stones of

God's temple, we must let ourselves be built up, by putting ourselves at the disposal of the builder.[21]

However, as much as the Spirit of God dwells in the Church and is the source of its creation, the Spirit can never be identified with the Church. The Holy Spirit is the Spirit of God and remains transcendent to all creation. This Spirit proceeds from God and through it God acts *in* the Church, reveals and communicates one's self *to* the community of the faithful. The Spirit permeates the Church but never becomes the Church's own spirit, nor merges with it. It remains God's own Spirit. Referring to the fundamental distinction between the Spirit of God and the Church, Hans Kung notes:

> This difference is not merely a general and abstract one, but the ontic difference between the divine and the human. The real Church, of which we are speaking, is not only a Church composed of people, but of sinful people. The real Church is not only human, but also sinful. We are the Church, justified but sinful men, we the fellowship of the righteous who are yet constantly dependent on forgiveness: *communio sanctorum* (communion of saints) indeed, but also regrettably always the *communio peccatorum,* (communion of sinners). So the Church is sinful. The Spirit of God on the other hand is not sinful, but the Holy, the completely Holy, Spirit.[22]

A self-understanding of the Church that overlooks the fundamental difference between the perfect Spirit of God and the imperfect Church, will fall prey to an idealistic and often triumphalistic conception of the Church, a conception which is full of illusions. A Church that identifies itself with God's eternal reality of the Spirit will eventually fall victim to idolatrous conceptions.

Furthermore, God's Spirit should never be identified with human potential. The Spirit is not in the idealistic sense, the spirit of human being, the knowing and willing self. It is neither an intellectual nor ethical principle; the Spirit is not the spirit of the age or a certain kind of consciousness. Kung states:

> The Spirit is no other than God *himself*: God close to man and the world, as comprehending but not comprehensible, self-bestowing but not controllable, life-giving but also directive power and force. He is then not a third party, not a thing between God and men, but God's personal closeness to men.[23]

Often God's Spirit has been misinterpreted as an obscure, nameless, divine power, or a sort of magical being of animistic character, while in the New Testament Spirit is God's ownself, gaining dominion over the mind and heart of people, becoming inwardly present to them and giving effective testimony to human soul.

In and through the Spirit, God gives oneself to the intellectual creature, and as the innermost life to humans. The giving of the personal Spirit of God has been called, in scholastic terms a *donum increatum*, God bestowing God's ownself upon human beings. But, God's self-giving carries with it also created gifts; God's supernatural communication effects created gifts of grace.[24] God's self-giving transforms the person that receives God's grace and love. God's self-giving, therefore, results in a created grace, which is a transformation effected in the person.

In relation to the created grace, it may be appropriate to briefly consider the concept of *charisms* referred to in the New Testament. The idea of *charis* (grace) in the New Testament points primarily to the totality of the saving plan of God executed in Jesus Christ by which humans are made righteous. However, in the New Testament a strong emphasis is also given on that which is given through grace. A special mission is a fruit of grace: Stephen was full of grace and power by which he spoke (Ac. 6:8). Paul speaks several times of his apostleship as a grace which he has received (Rm. 1:5; 12:3; 15:15; 1 Cor. 3:10; 15:10; Ga. 2:9; Eph. 3:7f). Grace fructifies in good works in the churches in Macedonia. *Charis* engenders *charismata*. Strictly speaking *charis* has to be distinguished from *charisma*, the favor granted by the former. Charisma is used to designate a particular type of spiritual gift which enables its receiver to perform a function in the Church. Hence a *charisma* should be called a sign of the triumph of grace, given for the service of the community.

Therefore, the *charisma* in the Church cannot be understood in any other way except within the context of God's Economy of selfgiving grace. The former should be regarded as resulting not from a purely exterior divine ordination, or from an external "decree" of God (as classicist theology presented it), but is to be counted as constitutive of grace.

The essential reality in Christian Economy is the reality of the divine mystery graciously operative in human history. The new dispensation of God's self-giving in Spirit and grace, differs from the legal or external system of the old dispensation. God is present not in temples made by hands, but in the people itself. The hour has truly come when the Father finds true worshipers in spirit and in truth, when he is to be worshipped no longer on Garizim or at Jerusalem. Every soul has become Jerusalem, a Temple of God, a living stone in a "spiritual" sanctuary.[25]

Jesus radically transformed the whole character of the worship of God. He did not simply replace the priesthood of Aaron by another priesthood, or the covenant and the temple, law and sacrifice of the Old Testament with another. He inaugurated a "newness" in virtue of the Incarnation and the gift of the Holy Spirit. The temple, the place of the presence of God is the community of the faithful, a spiritual house of living stones, wherein are offered spiritual sacrifices acceptable to God through the Risen Lord (1 Peter 2:5; cf 1 Cor. 3:10-17; Eph. 2:19-22; 4:11-16; etc.). The sacrifice, the priesthood, and the temple now are "spiritual," which does not mean metaphorical but corresponding to God's work in humans. They have been transposed into the moral realm, in a word, have become interior to humans. In the matter of sacrifice, for instance, the Divine Economy impels us to a state of things where the real sacrifice consists not in ritual doings, but in human being's self-giving to God. Thus, the "spiritual" character of the Christian system of worship derives from what is specific to the messianic era, which is the gift of the Holy Spirit.[26] Therefore, the essential and decisive reality of the Church is God's ownself being operative in the body of the faithful, a God who through the Spirit communes with the community of the faithful. All other things in the Church, such as sacraments, churches built of stone, laws and legal authority, are subordinate to that which is essential and definitive.

Furthermore, the Catholic tradition sees the transcendental reality of God in and through the categorical realities. No theological principle or focus is more characteristic of Catholicism than the principle of sacramentality, observes Richard McBrien. "The visible, the tangible, the finite, the historical--all these are actual or potential carriers of the divine presence. Indeed it is only in and through these material realities that we can even encounter the invisible God."[27] However, the failure to distinguish the sacramental reality from the transcendent reality itself, leads, first, to the denial of the ultimacy of God, reducing God to a categorical being, and thus drawing God to the level of the finite and conditional. Second, if sacramental realities are not recognized for their sacramental role, then there evolves the danger of identifying them with the transcendent reality and giving them an absolute character, falling thereby into idolatrous conceptions.

The Catholic tradition has strongly upheld the "sacramental" dimension of Christian economy. Unfortunately, sacramentality came to be narrowly referred to the seven sacraments of the Church, when in fact, sacramentality begins with the very historical realization of God's self-giving to humans. God's personal encounter with us was realized historically. God's self-giving in Spirit and grace had an outward embodiment in Jesus Christ, the primordial sacrament. Hence, sacrament in this wider sense, means "a divine bestowal of salvation in an outwardly perceptible form which makes the bestowal manifest; a bestowal of salvation in historical visibility."[28] Now God's self-communication in Spirit and grace continues to be operative in the Church; therefore, the

Church can be called the sacrament of salvation, i.e., the symbol signifying the reality of grace and at the same time participating in it,[29] but it can never be equated with the ultimate and absolute reality of God's own self.

Briefly, the God of Christian Economy is the God who gave onedelf in Spirit and grace, creating thereby a community, the Church. Hence, the essential and definitive reality of the Church is the reality of divine mystery graciously operative through spirit and grace in human history.   The   institutional Church, with its array of functions, organized worship, doctrines, moral codes and liturgical forms is called to signify the divine mystery. But any kind of identification of the institutional and symbolic aspects with the Divine Mystery itself, would amount to idolatry. The self- understanding of the Church becomes idolatrous when the institutional order of the Church is presented no longer as serving divine Mystery and Word, but equating itself with divine Mystery and Word.[30]

It is in view of this perspective of Christian Economy that we have to define the manner in which authority in the Church can become an authority of divine character, a grace-related and a grace-defined authority.

4. AUTHORITY AS THE POWER OF GRACE

According to Yves Congar, Jesus radically transformed the whole character and even the nature of authority; the Christian concept of authority is of a spiritual nature, "which does not mean metaphorical but corresponding to God's working in man."[31] Furthermore, it does not consist merely in the idea that authority must be exercised in a spirit of personal unselfishness and service, though of course this would lead to genuine and profitable developments. Authority is meant to be the result of the power of grace, the fruit of the indwelling of the Spirit.

In formulating a theory of authority in the Church we have to place it in the context of the Christian Economy. The latter is characterized by God's self-giving love in Jesus Christ. The foundational reality of Christian Economy is the reality of "God for us, God in touch with us, God with us, God bending down towards us, God given to us."[32] The visible Church is that permanent and visible expression of that economy of grace, of God's permanent presence among humans. As a community sustained by the Spirit of God, the Church is, therefore, epiphany of the sacred, "the consecrated reality, set apart to constitute the visibility of grace."[33] Hence, the concept of authority in the Church cannot be conceived after the likeness of a political entity, but has to be understood in relation to the transcendent spiritual principle. Any and every kind of authority in the Church has to be, in effect, the power of grace and love, the authority of the Spirit itself shining through human channels. Such authority is not confined to the official hierarchical structure alone; it is the type of authority to be found among those who are purely and simply godly persons. It is the authority present in those who are genuinely spiritual people and friends of God. Since the moral base of such authority is the reality of grace, the moral power that a spiritual person has is the power of God's grace operative in him or her. A theory of authority, if not founded upon the reality of God's self-communication in Spirit and grace, it runs the risk of suggesting a structure of merely socio-political nature, and distorting thereby the notion of authority, unique to the Church.

Congar points out that in the history of the Church, the period of the church of martyrs (spanning from the time of the apostles to the peace of Constantine) and the period of monastic christianity (from the fourth to the middle of the eleventh century) manifests the markedly spiritual character of the authority in the Church. Only those who were "men of God" had authority. Authority in the Church lay with those who were spiritually alive. The bishop in the early Church was a spiritual man endowed in a preeminent way with the gifts of the Spirit to lead God's people. If the goal in the Church is to form spiritual people, to introduce the souls to the "philosophy of Christ," then only those spiritually alive were regarded as capable of exercising authority over the faithful. Authority in the Church, in the final analysis, was the authority of the Spirit itself shining through the purity of *vir Dei*.[34] Ecclesiology was never divorced from spiritual anthropology.

But as a visible organization, the Church will have the need of a juridical structure, and an institutional governing organ. The juridical element, however, must derive its significance in subservience to the essential reality of the

Church, which is the reality of grace operative through God's Spirit. The institutional aspect is called to symbolize, and to be a sacrament of the power of grace and love. The juridical element ought to draw its theological significance in view of the "spiritual" reality of the Church, its essential reality.

In its essence the Church is a temple of God's presence. Through the Spirit, God is graciously operative in human history, and the community of the faithful is precisely the temple of God's dwelling. And the visible institutional aspect of the Church with its array of functions and organization is called to express and signify the mystery of grace operative in history. We may say therefore that the function of the institutional order is to "sacramentalize" the mystery of God's abiding presence; the institution is meant to symbolize and serve the mystery of grace.

In order to clarify the place and role of the juridical authority, it may be helpful to draw on an illustration that Jaroslav Pelikan uses in another context, in his work *The Vindication of Tradition*.[35] In the course of the iconoclastic controversies and the vigorous debate over the propriety of the use of images, a distinction evolved between an idol, a token, and a true image or icon. An "idol" purports to be the embodiment of that which it represents, but it directs us to itself rather than beyond itself. A "token" on the other hand, does point beyond itself, but it is altogether an accidental representation that does not embody what it represents. Finally, an authentic image, which came to be called "icon" in Greek, is what it represents; it bids us to look at it, but through it and beyond it, to that living reality of which it is an embodiment. Applying the above distinction to our issue, it appears that institutional authority became an *idol* when the authority of God came to be seen as physically and automatically present in the institution, or when the absolute standard of divine truth was identified with the ecclesiastical office, for it directed us to the institution rather than beyond itself. Institutional authority became a *token* in liberal Protestantism in which the overriding reality was personal interaction between the individual and God, and the institutional element was purely accidental. But if we accept that the Christian economy is historically operative, then the institutional reality should stand for an *icon*, which bids us to look at it, and through it to beyond it. It disclaims any identification with the authority of the Ultimate, but functions only as an embodied witness. Such ought to be, it seems, the place of the juridical element of the Church.

Since authority in the Church is fundamentally a power of grace. Such and authority goes beyond the boundaries of juridical power. Therefore, authority in the Church, is not a monopoly of the clergy, nor of juridically instituted offices.

We can briefly summarize the nature of authority and what it entails as follows:

a) Authority in the Church is of "spiritual" nature. Since the essential reality of the Church is God's self-communication in Spirit and grace, authority consists in the power of God's grace communicated to humans. God's self-giving carries a created gift with it, which consists in a transformation effected in the persons. God's self-giving is an effectual love which transforms the persons God loves.

b) Hence, authority cannot be confined to the governing activity of the ruling organ, for the reality of grace permeates the entire body and unfolds in varied and manifold ways. For instance, a prophet is not an officer, nor is he/she part of the official hierarchy. But as a prophet, he/she speaks with authority. He/she enjoys divine authority within the Church.

c) Since the Church is a visible institution, it requires an organizing juridical structure. The latter has to be understood as relative to, and expressive of, the reality of God's grace. The juridical realm ought to symbolize and serve the mystery of grace operative in the Church.

d) Those entrusted with juridical power need to realize the symbolic nature of their power. Their juridical power ought to draw its authority from the spiritual reality, the reality of grace operative in them. Only "godly persons," those spiritually alive, will be able to form spiritual people, to introduce people to the philosophy of Christ.

e) Evidently, the juridical power in the Church cannot be conceived as *dominium* (dominion) over the faithful, as in the understanding of civil authority. For the juridical element is called to signify the mystery of graced love, which in turn, leads to self-gift and service in a brotherly community.   In the midst of the faithful, the superior is *quasi unus ex illis* (like one of them). [36]

CONCLUSION

The authority in the Church is *sui generis*. Its theological articulation has to be based upon and drawn out from the essential reality of the Church. This does not mean that the Church will not adopt or produce new forms of authority to express its essential reality. There is nothing foreign to the nature of the Church in developing various forms of authority in order to adapt to changing needs. As John McKenzie observes:

> Evolution of form has been constant since the apostolic period. Weighed in the balance of history and theology, most of these forms appear to be phenomena which the Church produces and which the Church can take away. Some of them are better fitted to her mission, and some less fitted; some are suitable for certain periods and cultures, and unsuited to others. Authority is indestructible and incorruptible in the Church; the concrete forms in which authority appears do not share this incorruptibility[1]

The classicist view reduced authority to juridical power. In the course of history, the concept of *dominium* became central to the understanding of authority in the Church. With the definition of the Church as *societas perfecta*, the preoccupation with the rights and powers of the sacerdotal class over the rest of the faithful became paramount. By the time of Vatican Council I, the issue of the ruling power of the pope and the sacerdotal class took over the center stage in the life of the Church and in ecclesiology. The defensive posture adopted by the Church, especially since the Protestant Reformation, became ever more hardened in response to the intellectual and political movements in the nineteenth century, and it became petrified with the Modernist controversy. The Church felt its institutional authority was being threatened.

The Church then protected itself from the alleged assault on its additional authority first, by consolidating its structures by means of a greater centralization, and second, by providing a "mystique" for that structural power. The ruling ecclesiastical authority came to be identified and invested with the absolute standard of God's own authority. The institutional form of ecclesiastical authority came to be interpreted as, and completely identified with God's own will.

When a finite reality is thus elevated to be the ultimate measure, or when a human order makes claims for absolute truth, it amounts to sacralization. Sacralization assails God's transcendence and ultimacy and, by raising a finite reality to the order of the absolute, upholds idolatry. When the Church in its institutional order falls victim to sacralization, it forfeits its "sacramental" function and falls prey to idolatry. Religious absolutism is a form of idolatry, which not only implies a betrayal of Christian God, but is also inimical to humanity. A ruling bureaucracy, that sees its order of rule as the ultimate standard for Christian living, is a far cry from the central mystery of Christian Economy, that is, the salvific self-giving of God to humankind, realized in the person of Jesus of Nazareth, and now operative through Spirit and grace.

The Church however, as a visible organization, will be in need of a juridical structure, but the juridical element must be seen as serving the power of grace and love in the Church. The juridical power should be expressive of the power of God's grace and love and therefore it can never amount to a *dominium* of a privileged few over the rest, as in a secular understanding.

In the ecclesiology of Vatican Council II, the theme of the Church as an organized society or institution is clearly subordinated to those of the Church as mystery, sacrament, and communion of grace. Yet, notes Avery Dulles, "the image of the People of God, which holds a major position in the Constitution on the Church, is developed in such a way as to imply institutional and hierarchical structures."[2] The shift, writes Dulles, has been one of emphasis more than substance. Thus the institutional self-understanding has continued to retain its position of preeminence, and as a result, institutional dynamics of control and power will prevail in such ecclesiology. [3] And within such a model, Christianity can easily be reduced to an ideology supporting institutional self-interests, power relations or institutional controls under the guise of orthodoxy.

In order for the Church to live as a sign and sacrament of a redeemed humanity, it should manifest in visible fashion what the human community is meant to be. In particular, it should demonstrate that in Jesus Christ the subordinations created by a sinful world, by humanity's inherent greed for power and domination, have been overcome. For "there are no more distinctions between Jew and Greek, slave and free, male and female" (Gal. 3:28), since all are one in Christ Jesus, and all have been empowered in virtue of the Spirit, to call God "Abba, Father" (Gal. 4:6). Jesus radically transformed the nature of authority and, as a result, the authority in the Church cannot be founded on the power of dominion, but on the power of grace and the indwelling of the Spirit.

For, "You know that among the pagans the rulers lord it over them, and their great men make their authority felt. This is not to happen among you" (Mt. 20:25-26).

NOTES

INTRODUCTION

[1]Karl Rahner, et al. eds. *Sacramentum Mundi* (New York: Herder and Herder, 1968), s.v. "Absolutism" by Oskar Kohler.

[2]"History and the Church: A Mutual View," *Concilium* (1971), 68:31.

[3]Yves Congar, *Power and Poverty in the Church*, trans. Jennifer Nicholson (Baltimore: Helicon Press), 19.

[4]Oiknomia (economy) is a theological term used by Fathers of the Church to refer to God's activity in the world, particularly with reference to the Old Testament and New Testament dispensation.

[5]John McKenzie, *Authority in the Church* (Kansas City: Sheed and Ward, 1966; repritn 1985), 176-177 (page references are to reprint edition).

SECTION I: A HISTORICAL SURVEY

1. HISTORICAL CONTEXT

[1]Anthony Downs, *Inside Bureaucracy* (Boston: Little, Brown & Co., 1967).

[2]J. E. Lynch, "Co-responsibility in the First Five Centuries: Presbyteral Colleges and the Election of Bishops," paper presented at the Symposium on Co- responsibility in the Church, sponsored by the Canon Law Society of America, 1972. Quoted in Donald Warwick, "The Centralization of Ecclesiastical Authority: An Organizational Perspective," *Concilium,* 91 (1974): 111.

[3]Jaroslav Pelikan, *The Excellent Empire: The Fall of Rome and the Triumph of the Church* (San Francisco: Harper and Row Publishers, 1987), 25-26.

[4]Karl Baus, "The Development of the Church of the Empire within the Framework of the Imperial Policy," in *History of the Church*, ed. Hubert Jedin and John Dolan (New York: Seabury Press, 1980), 2:83.

[5]Ibid., 2:84.

[6]Ibid., 2:393-394.

[7]Ibid., 2:404.

[8]Ibid., 2:408.

[9]Jeffrey Richards, *The Popes and the Papacy in the Early Middle Ages: 476- 752* (London, Boston, Henley: Routledge & Kegan Paul), 12-15, 30.

[10]George H. Sabine, *A History of Political Theory*, 4th ed., (Hinsdale, Ill.: Dryden Press, 1937), 182-190.

[11]Hans-Georg Beck, "The Early Byzantine Church," in *History of the Church,* ed., Hubert Jedin and John Dolan (New York: Seabury Press, 1980), 2:420.

[12]Richards, *Popes and the Papacy*, 35.

[13]Ibid., 45.

[14]*Homiliae in Evangelia*, II. 6, 22, quoted in Richards, *Popes and the Papacy*, 47.

[15]J. B. Bury, *History of the Later Roman Empire,* (London: McMillan & Co., 1923), 62.

[16]Richards, *Popes and the Papacy*, 53.

[17]Eugen Ewig, "The Papacy's Alienation from Byzantium and Rap-prochment with the Franks," in *History of the Church*, ed. Hubert Jedin and John Dolan (New York: Crossroad Publishing, 1982), 3:4-95.

[18]Friedrich Kempf, "The Church and the Western Kingdoms from 900 to 1046," in *History of the Church*, ed. Hubert Jedin and John Dolan (New York: Crossroad Publishing, 1982), 3:280.

[19]Yves, Congar, Lay People in the Church (Westminster, Md.: Newman Press, 1956), 39.

[20]Walter Ullman, *Medieval Papalism* (London: Methuen & Co., 1948), 8.

[21]Source: All references from John J. Clarkson and others, *The Church Teaches*, (1955) have been reprinted by permission of the publisher, TAN Books and Publishers, Inc., 74; DS873.

[22]Yves Congar, *Power and Poverty*, 106.

[23]Yves Congar, *Lay People*, 29.

[24]Sabine, *History of Political Theory*, 313.

[25]Ibid., 313-318.

[26]Yves Congar, *Lay People*, 32.

[27]Ibid., 33.

[28]Ibid., 39.

[29]Ibid., 28.

[30]Ibid., 39.

[31]Congar, "The Historical Development of Authority in the Church. Points for Christian Reflection," in *Problems of Authority*, ed. J.M. Todd (Baltimore: Helicon, 1962), 140.

[32]Kenneth S. Latourette, *Christianity in a*

Revolutionary Age: a History of Christianity in the Nineteenth and Twentieth Centuries (New York: Harper and Brothers, 1958), 1:45.

[33]Ibid., 46.

[34]Ibid., 48-50

[35]Roger Aubert and others, "The Church in a Secularised Society," in *The Christian Centuries* (New York, Ramsey, N.J., Toronto: Paulist Press; London: Darton, Longman and Todd, 1978), 5:28.

[36]Latourette, *Christianity in A Revolutionary Age*, 1:238.

[37]Clarkson, *The Church Teaches*, 94-95; *DS* 3050-3052.

[38]Ibid., 102; *DS* 3072.

[39]Clarkson, *The Church Teaches*, 88.

2. CHURCH AS A BODY

[40]Michael Wilks, *The Problem of Sovereignty in the Later Middle Ages; the Papal Monarchy with Augustinus Triumphus and the Publicists* (Cambridge, England: Cambridge University Press, 1963), 19.

[41]Ibid., 46.

[42]Walter Ullman, *The Growth of Papal Government in the Middle Ages: A Study in the Ideological Relation of Clerical to Lay Power*

(London: Methuen, 1955), 273.

[43]Wilks, *Problem of Sovereignty*, 24.

[44]"Historical Development of Authority," 138.

[45]Frederick Copleston, *A History of Philosophy* Westminster, Md: Bewman Press, 1950), 2:413.

[46]Ullman, *Growth of Papal Government*, 290.

[47]Wilks, *Problem of Sovereignty*, 26.

[48]Yves Congar, *The Historical Development of Authority*, 144.

[49]For these and other modern encyclicals, see Claudia Carlen, ed., *The Papal Encyclicals* (Wilmington, N.C.: McGrath Publishing, 1981).

[50]Yves Congar, *Power and Poverty in the Church*, 109, trans. Jennifer Nicholson (Baltimore: Helicon Press, 1964)

3. AUTHORITY AS A POWER TO RULE

[51]R.W. Carlyle and A. J. Carlyle. *A History of Mediaeval Political Theory in the West.* (New York & London, 1930), 3:156.

[52]Ullmann, *Medieval Papalism*, 1-16.

[53]Clarkson, *Church Teaches*, 72-73; *DS* 861.

[54]Ibid., 75; *DS* 870-873.

[55]Ibid., 77-78; *DS* 1307.

[56]*Power and Poverty*, 103.

[57]Clarkson, *Church Teaches*, 84; *DS* 2888.

[58]Ibid., 85-86; *DS* 2895.

[59]Ibid., 93-94.

[60]Ibid., 95; *DS* 3053.

[61]Ibid., 95; *DS* 3055.

[62]Ibid., 98; *DS* 3060.

[63]Ibid., 99; *DS* 3064.

[64]*Power and Poverty*, 108.

[65]Henry Campbell Black, ed., *Black's Law Dictionary*, (St. Paul, Minn.: West Publishing Co., 1968, 4th ed.).

[66]Yves Congar, *Power and Poverty*, 60.

[67]*The Growth of Papal Government*, 45.

[68]Ibid., 286.

SECTION II: THEOLOGICAL REFLECTIONS.

1. A CRITIQUE OF THE TRADITIONAL VIEW OF AUTHORITY

[1]Mircea Eliade, *Cosmos and History: The Myth of the Eternal Return*, trans. Willard R. Trask (New York: Harper and Row, 1959), 34. Eliade states that Plato was the first to articulate and give philosophical currency to the cosmological world view.

[2]Ibid., 63.

[3]Ibid., 164.

[4]*Summa Theologica*, trans. Fathers of the English Dominican Province (New York, Boston, Cincinnati, Chicago, Sans Francisco: Benziger Brothers, 1947), I, Pt. I, QQ 103-119.

[5]Ibid., I, Pt. I, Q. 103, 5.

[6]Ibid., I, Pt. I, Q. 103, 7.

[7]Davis, *God's Grace*, 23.

[8]Davis, *God's Grace*, 30.

[9]*Religion and Alienation. A Theological Reading of Sociology*, (New York?Paramus/Toronto: Paulist

Press, 1975), 65.

2. THE DEMOCRATIC IDEAL

[10]David L. Sills, ed. *The International Encyclopedia of Social Sciences* (New York: The Macmillan Co. and The Free Press, 1968), IV, s.v. "Democracy," by Giovanni Sartori.

[11]Ibid., 4:112.

[12]Edward Schillebeeckx, "Christian Identity and Human Integrity," in *Concillium*, 155 (may 1982), 26.

[13]*Authority in the Church*, 16-17.

[14]Ibid., 176-177.

[15]*God's Grace*, 91.

3. THE CHRISTIAN ECONOMY

[16]Charles Davis, *God's Grace in History* (New York: Sheed and Ward, 1966), 54-55.

[17]*Theological Investigations*, trans. Cornelius Ernst, O.P. (Baltimore: Helicon Press; London: Darton, Longman & Todd, 1961), 1:310.

[18]Yves Congar, *The Mystery of the Temple or The*

Manner of God's Presence to his Creatures from Genesis to Apocalypse, trans. Reginald F. Trevett (Westminster, Md.: Newman Press, 1962), 238-248.

[19]Davis, *God's Grace*, 29-30.

[20]Yves Congar, *Mystery of the Temple*, 239-40.

[21]Hans Kung, *The Church*, trans. Ray and Rosaleen Ockenden (New York: Sheed and Ward, 1967), 170.

[22]Ibid., 174.

[23]Hans Kung, *On Being a Christian*, trans. Edward Quinn (Garden City, N.Y.: Doubleday, 1976), 469.

[24]I am following Karl Rahner's position, who, following patristic tradition, holds that created gift is the consequence of God's substantial communication (uncreated grace); while a prevalent scholastic position held that created grace is the condition for uncreated grace.

[25]Yves Congar, *Mystery of the Temple*, 240.

[26]Ibid., 149.

[27]Richard McBrien, *Catholicism* (San Francisco: Harper & Row Publishers, 1981), 1180.

[28]Edward Schillebeeckx, *Christ the Sacrament of Encounter with God* (London, Sydney: Sheed and Ward, 1963; reprint 1966), 15 (page references are

to reprint edition).

[29]Ibid., 253.

[30]Gregory Baum, *Religion and Alienation: A T Theological Reading of Sociology* (New York, Paramus, Toronto: Paulist Press, 1975), 64.

4. AUTHORITY AS A POWER OF GRACE

[31]*Power and Poverty*, 82.

[32]Yves Congar, The Historical Development of Authority, 122.

[33]Davis, *God's Grace*, 115.

[34]Yves Congar, *The Historical Development of Authority*, 123-127.

[35](Yale University Press, 1984), 55.

[36]Congar, Power and *Poverty*, 99.

CONCLUSION

[1]McKenzie, *Authority in the Chuch*, 13-14.

[2]Dulles, Avery, "A Half Century of Ecclesiology," in *Theological Studies*, 50 (September, 1989), 425.

[3]Ibid., 430.

SELECT BIBLIOGRAPHY

I list here only the writings that have been of use in the making of this book. This bibliography is by no means a complete record of all the works and sources available on the issue. It indicates the substance and range of reading upon which I have formed my ideas.

Aubert, Roger. "The Modernist Crisis and the 'Integrist' Reaction." In *The Christian Centuries, The Church in Secularised Society,* 5: 186-263. Ed. Louis J. Rogier et. al., London: Darton, Longman & Todd Ltd.: N. York: Paulist Press; Paris: Les Éditions du Seuil. Du Seuil, 1978.

Baum, Gregory. *Religion and Alienation. A Theological Reading of Sociology.* N. York/ Paramus/ Toronto: Paulist Press, 1975.

____ "Sociology and Theology." *Concilium* 91 (1974): 22-31.

____ *The Credibility of the Church Today: A Reply To Charles Davis.* New York, Herder & Herder, 1968.

Black, Henry Campbell, ed. *Black's Law Dictionary.* St. Paul, Minn.: West Publishing Co., 1968.

Blenkinsopp, Joseph. *Celibacy, Ministry, Church.* New York: Herder, 1968.

Bury, J. B. *History of the Later Roman Empire.* London: McMillan & Co.Ltd., 1923.

Carlen, Claudia. *The Papal Encyclicals.* New York: McGrath Publishing Company, 1981.

Carlyle, R. W. and A. J. *A History of Mediaeval Political Theory in the West.* New York and London. 6 vols. 1923-36.

Clarkson, John F. & Others, eds. *The Church Teaches.* St. Louis: B. Herder Book Co., 1955.

Congar, Yves. *Christians Active in the World.* Translated by P. J. Hepburne- Scott. New York: Herder & Herder, 1968.

____ "Church History as a Branch of Theology." *Concilium* 57 (1970): 85-96.

____ *L'Eglise.* Paris: Editions du Cerf, 1970.

____ "The Historical Development of Authority in the Church. Points for Christian Reflection". In *Problems of Authority*, ed. J. M. Todd, 119-156. Baltimore: Helicon, 1962.

____ *A History of Theology.* Translated and edited by

Hunter Guthrie. New York: Doubleday, 1968.

_____ *Laity, Church and World, Three Addresses.* Translated by Donald Attwater. London: G. Chapman, 1960.

_____ *Lay People in the Church: A Study for a Theology of Laity.* Translated by Donald Attwater. London: Bloomsbury Publishing, 1957.

_____ *The Mystery of the Church; Studies.* Translated by A. V. Littledale. Baltimore: Helicon Press, 1960.

_____ *The Mystery of the Temple; or The Manner of God's Presence to his Creatures from Genesis to the Apocalypse.* Translated by Reginald F. Trevett. Westminster, Md.: Newman Press, 1962.

_____ *Power and Poverty in the Church.* Translated by Jennifer Nicholson.Baltimore: Helicon, 1964.

_____ "The Sacralization of Western Society in the Middle Ages". *Concilium* 47 1969: 55-71.

Copleston, Frederick C. *A History of Medieval Philosophy.* (A revision and enlargement of *Medieval Philosophy* published in 1952). London: Methuen, 1972.

_____ *A History of Philosophy.* Westminster, Md.: Bewman Press, 1950.

Crehan, Joseph. "More Tyrrell Letters--1." *The Month* 226 (October 1968): 178- 85

Davis, Charles. *God's Grace in History.* New York: Sheed & Ward, 1966.

Denzinger, Heinrich. *Enchiridion symbolorum, definitionum et declarationum de rebus fidei et morum.* ed. Karl Rahner and Adolf Schonmetzer. Barcelona:

Herder, 1965.

Dix, Gregory. *Jurisdiction in the Early Church, Episcopal and Papal.* London: Faith House, 1975.

Downs, Anthony. *Inside Bureaucracy.* Boston: Little, Brown, 1967.

Dru, Alec. "Modernism and the Present Position of the Church." *Downside Review* 82 (April 1964): 103-10.

Dulles, Avery. *The Dimensions of the Church; a Postconciliar Reflection.*Westminster, Md.: Newman Press, 1967.

_____"A Half Century of Ecclesiology." In *Theological Studies* 50 (September 1989): 419-42.

_____ *A History of Apologies.* London, Hutchinson, 1971.

_____ *Models of the Church.* Garden City, New York: Doubleday, 1974.

_____ *Revelation Theology: A History.* New York: Seabury Press, 1969.

Fransen, Peter. "The Authority of the Councils." In *Problems of Authority,* ed. J. M. Todd. 43-78. Baltimore: Helicon, 1962.

Hasenhuttl, Gotthold. "Church and Institution." *Concilium* 91 (1974): 11-21.

Jedin, Hubert and John Dolan, eds. *History of the Church.* New York: Herder and Herder, Seabury Press, Crossroad, 9 vols., 1965-82.

Kantorowicz, Ernst H. *The King's Two Bodies. A Study in Medieval Political Theology.* Princeton University Press, 1957.

Kennedy, Eugene C. *Comfort My People; The Pastoral Presence of the Church,* New York: Sheed & Ward, 1968.

_____ *The People are the Church.* New York: Doubleday, 1969.

_____ *Tomorrow's Catholics, Yesterday's Church: The Two Cultures of* American Catholicism. New York: Harper & Row, 1988.

Knitter, Paul. "Christianity as Religion: True and Absolute? A Roman Catholic Perspective." *Concilium* 136 (1980): 12-21.

Knox, Wilfred Lawrence and Vidler, Alec R. *The Development of Modern Catholicism.* London: Philip Allan, 1933.

Kohler, Oskar. "Absolutism." In *Sacramentum Mundi,* eds. Karl Rahner et al., New York: Herder and Herder, 1968.

Kung, Hans. *The Church.* Translated by Ray and Rosaleen Ockenden. New York, Sheed & Ward, 1967; London: Burns & Oates, 1967.

_____ *On Being a Christian* Translated by Edward Quinn. Garden City, N.Y.: Doubleday, 1976.

Latourette, Kenneth S. *Christianity in a Revolutionary Age: a Historyof Christianity in the Nineteenth and Twentieth Centuries.* New York: Harper & Brothers, 1958.

_____ *Etude Historique.* Paris: Aubier, 1949.

Lubac, Henri de. *Catholicism: A Study of Dogma in Relation to the Corporate Divinity of Mankind.* Translated from the 4th french edition by Lancelot C.

Sheppard. London: Burns & Oates, 1950.

McBrien, Richard P. *Do We Need the Church?* New York, Harper & Row; London: Collins, 1969.

_____ *Catholicism.* San Francisco: Harper & Row Publishers, 1981.

McCool, Gerald. *Catholic Theology in the 19th Century. The Quest for a Unitary Method.* New York: Seabury, 1977.

McKenzie, John L. SJ. ed., *Dictionary of the Bible.* Milwaukee: The Bruce Publishing Co., 1965.

_____ *Authority in the Church.* Kansas City: Sheed and Ward, 1966; reprint 1985.

Neuner, Josef. "The Idea of Catholicity- Concept and History." In *The Church: Readings in Theology,* 61-92. New York: P.J. Kennedy, 1963.

Neuner, Josef & H. Roos. *The Teaching of the Catholic Church.* Staten Island, N. York: Alba House, 1967.

Ozment, Steven. *The Age of Reform 1250-1550.* Yale University Press, 1980.

Pelikan, Jaroslav. *The Excellent Empire: The Fall of Rome and the Triumph of the Church.* San Francisco: Harper & Row Publishers, 1987.

_____ *The Vindication of Tradition.* Yale University Press, 1984.

_____ *Primacy of the Person in the Church.* A series of five lectures at first annual Fides Forum held at Notre Dame University. Notre Dame: Fides Publishers, Inc., 1967.

Poulat Emile. "History and the Church: A Mutual View." *Concilium* 67 (1971): 17-32.

Rahner, Karl. "Christology Within an Evolutionary View of the World."*Theological Investigations* 5: 157-92. Translated by Karl H. Kruger. Baltimore: Helicon; London: Darton, Longman & Todd, 1966.

_____ *The Dynamic Element In the Church.* Translated by W. J. O'Hara. London: Burns & Oates. New York: Herder & Herder, 1964.

_____ *Foundations of Christian Faith: An Introduction to the Idea of Christianity.* Translated by William V. Dych. London: Darton, Longman &Todd, 1978; New York: Seabury, 1978.

_____ "Freedom In the Church." *Theological Investigations* 2: 89-107. Translated by Karl-H. Kruger. Baltimore: Helicon, 1963. London:Darton, Longman & Todd, 1963.

_____ Hearers of the Word. Translated by Michael Richards. New York: Herder & Herder, 1969.

_____ "The Historicity of Theology." *Theological Investigations* 9: 64-82. Translated by Graham Harrison. New York: Herder & Herder, 1972.London: Darton, Longman & Todd, 1972.

_____ "History of the World and Salvation-History." *Theological Investigations* 5: 97-114. Translated by Karl-H. Kruger. Baltimore: Helicon; London: Darton, Longman & Todd, 1966.

_____"The New Claims Which Pastoral Theology Makes Upon Theology As a Whole." *Theological Investigations* 11: 115-36. Translated by David Bourke. New York: Seabury; London: Darton, Longman & Todd, 1974.

____"On the Theology of the Incarnation." *Theological Investigations* 4: 105-20. Translated by Kevin Smyth. Baltimore: Helicon; London:Darton, Longman & Todd, 1966.

____ "The Teaching Office of the Church in the Present-Day Crisis of Authority." *Theological Investigations* 12: 3-30. Translated by David Bourke. New York: Seabury; London: Darton, Longman & Todd, 1974.

____ "Theology and Anthropology." *Theological Investigations* 9: 28-45 Translated by Graham Harrison. New York: Herder & Herder. London:Darton, Longman & Todd, 1972.

____"Theology and the Church's Teaching Authority After the Council." *Theological Investigations* 9: 83-100. Translated by Graham Harrison. New York: Herder & Herder; London: Darton, Longman & Todd, 1972.

____ "Theology of Freedom." *Theological Investigations* 6: 178-196. Translated by Karl H. and Boniface Kruger. Baltimore: Helicon Press; London: Darton, Longman & Todd, 1969.

Richards, Jeffrey. *The Popes and the Papacy in the Early Middle Ages:* 476-752. London, Boston & Henly: Routhledge & Kegan, Paul, 1979.

Sabine, George H. *A History of Political Theory*. Hinsdale, Illinois: Dryden Press, 4th ed., 1973.

Sanks, Howland. *Authority in the Church: A Study in Changing Paradigms*. Missoula, Mont.: Scholars' Press, 1974.

Schillebeeckx, Edward. *God the Future of Man*. Translated by N. D. Smith. New York: Sheed & Ward, 1968.

_____ *Christ the Sacrament of Encounter with God.* London, Sydney: Sheed & Ward, 1966.

_____ "Christian Identity and Human Integrity." *Concilium* 155 (May 1982): 23-31.

Sills, David L., ed. "Democracy." In *The International Encyclopedia of Social Sciences.* New York: The Macmillan Co. and The Free Press, 1968.

Todd, John M., ed.. *The Historical Development of Authority; Problems of Authority.* Baltimore: Helicon Press, 1962.

Ullman, Walter. *The Growth of Papal Government in the Middle Ages; a Study in the Ideological Relation of Clerical to Lay Power.* London: Methuen, 1955.

_____ *Medieval Papalism.* London: Methuen, 1948.

Warwick, Donald. "The Centralization of Ecclesiastical Authority: An Organizational Perspective." *Concilium* 91 (1974): 109-118.

Wilbur, Marshall Urban. *Humanity and Deity.* London: George Allen & Unwin Ltd., 1951.

Wilks, Michael. *The Problem of Sovereignty in the Later Middle Ages.* Cambridge University Press, 1963.

ABOUT THE AUTHOR

Meneo A. Afonso is an Assistant Professor in the Philosophy and Religious Studies Department at Cardinal Stritch College, Milwaukee. He holds an M.A. in Eastern and Western Philosophy, and a Ph. D. in Religious Studies. His scholarly interests include the philosophical school of thought in personalism, and the area of spiritual anthropology.